More
Monday
Morning
Musings
*Reflections from the
Principal's office*

More
Monday
Morning
Musings

*Reflections from the
Principal's office*

C. A. Kilgallon

Illustrations by Leticia Monroe

For Donna —
With gratitude
C A Kilgallon
3/3/15

More Monday Morning Musings:
Reflections from the Principal's Office.

Copyright © 2008-2011 by C. A. Kilgallon.

Cover photograph by C. A. Kilgallon.
Illustrations by Leticia Monroe
Book Design by Melissa Mykal Batalin.

The Troy Book Makers • Troy, NY • thetroybookmakers.com

ISBN: 978-1-61468-040-6

Contents

Introduction

I write because I have to. It is as simple as that. Writing has become a part of who I am. The thing is, I have come to see words as a kind of tonic that I must consume each day to preserve my mental and spiritual health. I try to begin each day and end the day by reading from a book of fiction or non-fiction. The ideas contained in these varied works act as the kindling that will help ignite a fire of ideas that burn themselves onto the pages of the essays I produce each week.

Reading has become a life long exercise while the writing has come to acquire a place in my existence rather recently. Hopefully, as I have done with many authors, the reader of these brief essays will find a grain of truth that they can incorporate into their daily lives. Perhaps something written will spark a desire to think deeply about an issue or to explore the work of a mentioned author. The important part will be the connections that are made between the reader and the writer.

So, thank you reader, for taking the time to join in this adventure. I would welcome your feedback on these pieces. Through our dialogue we can hopefully find those connections that will enrich both our lives.

C.A. Kilgallon
July, 2011

September 8, 2008

The beige lace curtains fluttered on a soft warm July breeze, brushing against the mahogany stained window sill. The early morning sun threw bright beams of light over my cereal bowl while the train whistle blew in a distance, signaling the start of another summer day. After forty years these memories are still etched in my mind like carvings on the inside of ancient caves. A long time ago I spent many happy times at my grandparents upstairs flat in the Port Schuyler section of Watervliet.

In those days the concept of central air conditioning did not exist in private homes, so to get respite from the afternoon heat you simply darkened the rooms and settled for the screen filtered air to blow through. You hoped for a breeze, with the big box fan used for comfort around dinner time. I can still picture my grandfather in his sleeveless white undershirt serving up our meals in the blue willow patterned dishes accompanied by tall glasses of fresh lemonade.

At around seven o'clock when all the dishes were washed and put away we headed down to the small front porch. The custom was pretty much known as "stoop sitting". There really wasn't much to it. We took our three aluminum lawn chairs with the green and white stripped webbing, out from the hallway, and sat until darkness enveloped us and the mosquitoes came calling for their last evening snack. My grandparents read the afternoon edition of the newspaper and I was content to watch the sun creep slowly down toward the western horizon.

We did not have portable televisions, cell phones or ipods. Perhaps we may have engaged in simple conversations with the neighbors passing by on an evening stroll. Usually the conversation centered on the weather. It was simple, straight forward and very friendly. For sure, it would not have occurred to anyone to pass by without at least saying, "good evening". How times have changed!

Today it is certainly possible to live on a block and not even know your neighbors, let alone speak to them everyday. Embedded in our own technological self-contained wonderlands we often see conversation as distracting and intruding. Noise levels around our homes over power the ability of silence to calm frazzled nerves. Riding mini-tractor lawn mowers, power leaf blowers and gasoline propelled hedge trimmers pollute our domains with their noxious fumes and add to the girth of our waistlines.

If you had to literally do nothing for a few hours could you do it? Would you consider being in the moment a giant waste of time? How well do you tolerate silence? Do you find yourself running away from it with a sense of fear? I believe the ability to embrace silence is a prerequisite for a sane life.

Each year, when summer draws to an inevitable close, I stop and think of those quiet moments spent "stoop sitting" so long ago. The folding aluminum chairs are gone as well as the five cent blue raspberry popsicles I used to look forward to on those sweltering summer nights. However, the importance of sitting quietly and enjoying the peace of this short, wonderful season in the Northeast is with me still. It, too, is etched in the lines of the caverns of my mind.

This week try to carve out a few minutes of silence for yourself. As we transition into a new school year the demands of the days have a way of placing an ever increasing burden of stress upon us. It is easy to get caught up in a whirlwind of noise and distraction. So find a quiet corner and cultivate your own form of sitting practice. The "time out of mind" theory should not be ignored! Have a great week filled with the promise of the chance to begin this new venture together. We will do great things for all our learners if we just remember to take care of ourselves, too.

September 15, 2008

I noticed her at the airport in Albany. She was an attractive woman, possibly of Indian descent, probably in her late twenties. Impeccably dressed, she had a silver Coach handbag with matching silver slip-on shoes. Ready to board a flight to Charlotte, North Carolina, she was traveling with her husband. One other companion traveler of note accompanied her. It was a well worn gray colored teddy bear which she held just above the handbag. The little fellow appeared to be at least as old as the woman with a significant patch of missing fur around his forehead and paws. The sight of the creature brought a smile to my face in addition to a silent affinity with its' owner, a complete stranger.

In the course of our lifetimes we probably all develop a kinship with some sort of talisman or symbol that brings us a feeling of comfort. My talisman, as far back as I can remember, has been the teddy bear. I may have inherited this from my father who always spoke of the stuffed bears with much admiration. In fact, I recall several conversations about a childhood bear of his named Willie. It had been with him since boyhood and had all the markings of a loyal companion including several lines of black stitches across his body. A well worn nose, bald spots and floppy arms sealed his fate. Eventually I believe

Willie made his way to the teddy bear graveyard.

My first recollection of having to part with a cherished furry creature comes from my memory bank at about three years of age. I was walking with my parents just around the corner from our home. As we were strolling down the street I distinctly remember clutching my favorite brown teddy bear in one of my hands. Joy quickly turned to terror as a big Irish setter dog came charging up to us and snatched the bear right out of my hand. He ran away with the bear engulfed between his jaws and into his backyard. I remember sobbing at the top of my lungs at this act of unprovoked violence. Having been the victim of this terrible act, to this day I am leery of the Irish setter breed of dog. My father went up to the house in hopes of retrieving my little companion but, alas, the shredding had already been completed. I then entered a full fledged depression and grieved many days after that. In no time I am sure my parents went to the Montgomery Ward department store in an attempt to

replace my loss. To this day the thought of being without a teddy bear is simply unimaginable.

In my home I have a room that is surrounded by book shelves. The far corner of the room houses a pine and glass curio case which holds my prize bears including several 100 year anniversary commemorative bears. Along the tops of the book shelves the bears sit as sentinels guarding the hundreds of books that sit on those shelves. The bears are all unique in color, design and origin. Many of the bears were birthday or Christmas gifts. Some, such as a favorite black bear from Mt. Rainier, were chosen while traveling. Others are old, faithful companions, often embedded with my tears from sad occasions. The ones that were not gifts were chosen because of the appearance of their faces. All great teddy bear lovers know that the secret of choosing the best bear involves staring at the face of a bear for several minutes. Mouth, nose, and especially eyes have to align just right.

I love giving bears as gifts. They can give the greatest comfort and are the most reliable of creatures, In other words, you can always trust a teddy bear. I have given them to newborns and to ninety year olds and no one has ever wanted to return them. Maybe if more people kept their childhood teddy bears into adulthood we would have a better adjusted species walking around.

There is not much one can be sure of in this crazy world of ours. The times we live in can be unsettling at best. However, when I think of that woman in the airport carrying her teddy bear on board I take comfort. It just proves that my theory might be correct. Teddy bears do not disappoint. They are friends for all ages. With a teddy bear sitting next to you your chances to come out all right seem to improve. So you might want to make a trip up into your attic. If you are lucky you may find your old friend buried in a trunk. Just how precious would that be?

This week, as the subtle changes in the leaves remind us that summer will not last forever, take a moment to stop and think. Here at School 18 we all need to hang on to each other as we begin our new adventure this year. If we do this honorably, we can look back in June with real pride at our ability to be good bears!!!!!!!!!! Have a great week.

September 22, 2008

It is only when we feel powerless to make a difference that the creeping sensation of stagnation wisps us away and resignation sets in. One cannot help but despair at the condition of the world today. It is ripe with global warfare, violent acts of national and community rage and a general feeling of malaise. It seems that every segment of life has been invaded by a trend toward diving ever lower toward a collective vision of hell on earth that has been written about through the ages. While I cannot deny the existence of a depressive atmosphere I choose to believe that each person has the ability to influence the world in a positive manner. It is true, I believe, in no uncertain terms, that the global change begins with the dawning of each new day. The ability to add to the collective pain or to take a piece of it away begins when our feet touch the ground upon rising. To live with sheer integrity demands a series of choices that only the individual can make. Power, the authentic variety, is derived from the ability to interact in a positive manner with every human and non human encounter we have daily. The helplessness we feel to affect change is, in essence, a myth. If each individual practiced this kind of purposeful interaction we could all live a better life.

Think of all the tiny encounters you have before leaving

for work in the morning. Do you choose to treat yourself to a nutritious breakfast or do you just chow down a pastry loaded with sugar? If so, aren't you choosing to add to the collective pain by dishonoring the sacredness of your body? Do you choose exercise or another hour of sleep? What about your first encounters with your pets? Do you leave enough time to get ready with intent or do you hurriedly throw your clothes on and fly out the door with just enough time to reach your destination? I don't believe we give thought to the way we begin our days thus adding to the chaos of the world before we even head out the door!

In our arrogance, we forget that life is so fragile and we end up simply going on automatic pilot through the days which turn out to be years. Very few of us are educated to think and act with a sense of purpose. It matters greatly to our collective health that we make choices that are meaningful. We delude ourselves into believing that making money and having status is a sure fire way to be happy. That is the biggest myth around! Making good choices each day puts us on the path toward conscious living which brings us a sense of peace which equals happiness. That is as simple as it gets. Easy to say but hard to practice. We cling to anything that gives us approval and disregard the power of humility.

The animal kingdom has so much to teach us but we look down on the natural world as something we should dominate. It is rare to study the ways of nature as a source of personal inspiration. We think the only route is through self-help books and psychoanalysis when the smart thing to do is to sit in the woods and simply observe the great teachers at work. In so many ways thinking is overrated! As it has been said many times before, silence is a practice to be cultivated throughout our lives. People who are secure in themselves do not need to constantly babble on like raging rivers. A sublimely flowing brook can teach us the lesson of going slow, talking less and choosing well. Peace of spirit will not be found in the canyons of the mind, it will be found in the small crevices out of sight of the chatter that passes for conversation.

It is all a matter of choice, simple choice. Are we consciously making deliberate, well thought out choices or are we willing to approve the self-destructive path we are on? Does anyone care? Is "choice work" worth the effort? I strongly believe it is essential to the continuation of life. We all share the responsibility for leaving this world a better place. The question we need to ask at the end of each and every day is this, "Did I choose today to contribute to the pain or did I choose to take a bit of it away?" That fundamental question is one we must all face. We can pray for a better world or we can make it a better world through every interaction. It is up to us. It is a simple choice. That is the true power we were endowed with when we came to dwell here on this planet. Are you up to making your time here really count? Your choice!!!!!!

September 29, 2008

Fall is definitely in full swing. The morning air has that crisp chill to it and the dilemma becomes when to actually turn the heat on for the season. Every year I set a goal of October 1st but usually succumb to the final days of September. It is kind of like a game to see if I can tough it out but when I think of putting a polar fleece over a sweater in the house then I know the gig is up. Besides, it is no fun when the towels don't quite seem to dry completely after their morning workout. There seems to be a hint of dampness that just hangs around as a temptation to fire up the furnace. Every year I think that somehow Mother Nature will get fooled and just maybe summer can linger on into the first few weeks of October but, alas, my whims take second place to the march of a higher power and the frost appears right on schedule to usher in the days of decreasing daylight. Such a shift really lets us little humans know that we are not the boss of all!!

The loss of light does not appeal to my senses much but the arrival of apple pie season sort of makes up for the surrender a bit. Upstate New York and New England take center stage as the apple pie ritual continues through Thanksgiving time. The apple crop is coaxed down from the trees and the wonderful splendor begins to take shape. White sacks of gleaming red apples are toted home to await the peeling and chopping that sets the stage for the luscious finished product. Those of us who would rather skip the labor intensive part gather round the bakery case to inhale the pies just out of the oven, warm and bubbling.

Apple pies are interesting things to contemplate. They have universal appeal and it seems every cook has a variation on the theme so to speak. All varieties of apples go into making the pies with the sweet/tart combination left up to the desire of the baker. I have thought about the differences in apple pies for a long time. How come an item made with the same basic ingredient can come out tasting so totally different? There could be hundreds of pies all with a flavor not quite like the last one you sampled. What happens here? Generally, crust is crust and apples are apples. The difference is in the spices that are used! A glorious symphony of just the right tweaking of cinnamon, nutmeg and maybe a pinch of cloves yields

a moment of pure pleasure when you can just taste that maybe there is hope for a weary world. It is hard to be grumpy when you have just bitten into a big piece of fresh out of the oven apple pie.

As it goes with apple pies, maybe it goes with life. The secret might just lie in what kind of spices we put into our daily life creations. Basically, we all are made up of the same raw ingredients. One can live a very honorable life using those ingredients day by day. Perhaps a tad on the bland side, but sturdy and trustworthy just the same. However, to really soar in this life you have to add a liberal dose of just the right blend of spices. My list of those would include: compassion, a great sense of humor, humility, the ability to laugh at yourself, simplicity, knowing when to keep your mouth shut and a sense of wonder. Cover all that with a crust of integrity and you have the recipe for one good life!!

This week as we bid good-bye to the gateway month of September, think a little bit about your own version of a recipe for a great life. What are your favorite spices? This exercise is probably best accomplished when sitting by a warm crackling fire eating a big piece of apple pie and drinking a tall glass of milk. It almost makes the inevitable approach of winter just a tad more bearable. Best wishes for a great week filled with possibility! Thank you for coming here each day ready to be your best self as we strive to do this worthy work.

October 6, 2008

Well over 150 years ago a sage by the name of Henry David Thoreau preached the gospel of simplicity from his abode in Concord, Massachusetts. He was convinced that the authentic life was predicated on the ability to forego the trappings of a materialistic lifestyle. His two year experiment of living in a small cabin on the shores of Walden Pond proved that, indeed, less can be more. Even in 1840's New England Thoreau knew that the direction everyday life was taking spelled disaster for the necessity of living a balanced life. His desire to "check out" for a while gave him a unique perspective to comment on the ability of living an unbalanced life to ravage the spirit and throw the psyche into a state of constant stress. His tale of the adventure, <u>Walden.</u> has become for me the bible of sanity and I return to it when I feel on the precipice of a spiritual train wreck.

Even though the idea of running off to a cabin in the woods appeals to my desire to rid myself of the frantic pace of life, this is a rather unpractical solution at best. So, then, how does one put one's life into a grounded state? Can we keep one foot in the harried world and one foot in the world of stillness? It seems that our perceived need to be connected to everything and everyone at every minute of the day has robbed us of the need to "check out" both physically and mentally. The speed at which we are forced to live our lives is slowly, but surely, grinding us down into "human doings". We have no notion of how to achieve a state of "being" that leaves us in a place of contented bliss. We have come to equate slowing down with laziness and unproductivity. In losing the ability to simply observe the wonder of the world at our feet we have severed the chord that links us to the lessons that only nature can provide. All our materialistic strivings do is to cut us loose like a tethered balloon suddenly whisked away and set on a course spinning toward the blackness of space. We are collectively withdrawing into what we think is the safety of our own homespun cocoons. In essence, we fail to take the time in solitude to know our inner selves well enough to know that the pace at which we live our lives is destroying us from the inside out. The emptiness is chilling.

One answer to this dilemma is to cultivate the practice of listening. You cannot listen deeply if all your senses are in a heightened state of alert. So try to take a few moments each day to simply just <u>listen.</u> You will be surprised at the sounds you can actually hear! Think of how the animals in the wild actually use their sense of hearing just to stay alive.

Henry Thoreau's advice for us to "simplify, simplify" is still at the heart for the search to live an authentic life. In 2008 it is more than a piece of advice. Realistically, it is a warning. If we do not heed the call on some level we will self-destruct, leaving behind nothing but a trail of broken spirits. We are fast becoming a people with no soul. Before it is too late we need to reconnect with the prophets like Henry Thoreau who through some beautiful pieces of writing, tried to warn us of the dangers of our self indulgent ways. We are fools if we do not stop to listen to his voice calling out to us from the wind, the water and the trees. It is simple. Slow down, quiet down; the voices of story, the voices of wisdom are trying to speak to you. Can you hear them?

October 20, 2008

There is a great little cartoon from "Peanuts" by Charles Schultz dated 1996. In it Linus is relaxing on his ever present faithful blanket when Snoopy plops down beside him. Linus bemoans the appearance of the beagle but finds him having to admit that Snoopy is "kind of warm and fuzzy". In response, the four-legged philosopher responds, "everyone brings something to the party". Talk about the ability to cut to the chase and get to the core of one of life's fundamental truths! Snoopy totally gets it.

We are all here together on this planet. Some are better off than others; some have a difficult road to tread while some are seemingly blessed with endless good fortune. Nevertheless, we all find ourselves in this fast fading year of 2008 at the party we call life. What we sometimes fail to recognize is that everyone indeed brings something to the party. Each encounter we have each day brings the opportunity to recognize this fact and to place it at the center of our focus. Well, in theory this is so but what about in practice?

Those of us who find ourselves coming to places we call schools have a special chance to fine tune the "party" philosophy each and every single day. We are surrounded by quirky kids, unique colleagues and often challenging parents. Sometimes it just amounts to one messy stew. It is easy to get caught up in a tide of cynicism and to feel the grip of reality slowly loosening. There are days when it might be wise to bring a blanket to school just for security purposes. Maybe it is not so wise to give these things up. Linus may have a point in refusing to submit to his sister Lucy's constant threats to take away his blanket.

We yearn for stability, a sense that everything should proceed on an even keel. Sometimes maybe we even look back on our childhoods when it seemed like schools were the great fortresses of conformity and allegiance. In other words, do we subscribe to the "good old days" theory? Well, maybe that was a different time but I am not so sure it was a better time. I am beginning to think that different is a really good way to be. Most importantly, different might be a great way to teach. Do we want conformist clones or evolved, passionate thinkers who will not walk blindly into the chaotic abyss we now find ourselves entangled in on October 20, 2008? As educators, all of us in this building must ask ourselves that important question.

It comes back to honoring the idea that each child and each adult at School 18 brings something to the party. It might not be the gift that WE wanted them to bring, but that is the point. What makes this school tick is not sameness, it is difference. The challenge for us becomes how to honor those differences. Our task is to find the spirit that each person holds and nurture it so it is free to flourish. Yes, it would be easier on some days to just teach to the mean and to not have to get the dirt under our fingernails. But think about it, isn't teaching sometimes as complicated and as messy as performing brain surgery? Split second decisions can affect the outcome of a life. One wrong cut to someone's ego can literally change the course of what that person may accomplish. Children are like butterflies, totally spontaneous and free until someone decides to put a net over them.

So, this week as you set the table so to speak, take a few minutes to reflect on a very important question. In whatever role you play here at School 18, how will you honor the gifts that we all bring to the party?

Best wishes for a great week!!

October 27, 2008

It seems that Fall has officially arrived. There is always the hope that Summer will be able to pull off some kind of meteorological coup and the great weather will prevail until December. However, after this week it is abundantly clear that dreams will not come true this year. The damp rain of mid-week made a statement, pure and simple, that winter is gearing up and will soon descend upon us. The leaves have that distinctive crunch underfoot and the skies hold the remains of smoke expelled from chimneys fired up and ready to keep the chill at bay.

As the month of October winds to its climatic close, the main event is almost upon us. Halloween will dawn on Friday to mixed reviews I am sure. It has become the holiday people either love or hate. In our politically correct culture Halloween has taken many hits, many of which I believe are undeserved. At the core of this day is the simple truth that Halloween provides a day of magic for the little beings of the world. The symbolism of it and other assorted theories might best be left for the adults to contemplate. The opportunity to dress up as a favorite character and to engage in some fantasy for a day could just be a welcome respite for kids. We all know how much "reality", including graphic TV shows, has taken over our lives. Granted, the violence themed costumes are offensive but they are of recent vintage.

As a kid, I looked forward to Halloween. It was especially appealing in that, being Catholic school students, we always had the day after Halloween off in observance of All Saints' Day. We would begin our preparations after school let out. Our costumes were mostly home-made concoctions we dreamed up months before. They could be as simple as a white sheet draped over our heads, "Charlie Brown" style. As darkness descended, we headed out in search of some great treats. The trick part never entered our consciousness. Our carved pumpkin was placed on the porch with a glowing candle plopped in the center to act as a sentinel awaiting our safe return. We scurried around the neighborhood going door to door with our parents not far behind. Yes, there was a time family fun did not involve the mall and a hundred dollar bill!

Hitting the jackpot on Halloween for us meant getting a stash of five-cent Hershey bars. Nowadays, these gems go for about a dollar. We would return home after about an hour to cider and cookies. The loot was dumped out on the living room floor and separated into piles of keepers and those unwrapped pieces relegated to the trash can. Our rationed catch lasted at least to Thanksgiving. It was kind of empowering to come home from school each day and to look forward to picking out a candy bar. Choice is a powerful thing and isn't it nice to think that joy can come to a kid in the form of a simple piece of chocolate. Funny how some things don't change as we age.

My all-time favorite Halloween adventure had to be the year I dressed up as "Fearless Fly". I don't know what it says about my psychological state of mind to admit that I was once enamored of a character that fashioned itself after a common house fly. However, to my pint-sized little self, "Fearless Fly" was the epitome of cool. He carried an attache case made out of some kind of reflective material that housed a radio transmitter inside. His cape flew in the wind as he traversed the skies keeping all below safe and sound. I fashioned my cape out of an old sheet but my pride and joy that October was the case. I conned my mom into letting me have a coat box with a plastic handle that opened and I went to town. After conjuring up a sleek black mask and draping it over my eyes I was ready to protect the whole neighborhood.

The "fearless" part was not the problem. As a kid there was not much I was afraid of. The second part of the equation proved to be a bit more challenging. Somehow I got the brainstorm to attempt the "fly" part. I ascended to the top of the attic stairs and frankly, to this day, don't know what I was thinking. The next thing I knew I was flat out at the bottom of the stairs seeing stars even though it was mid-day. Needless to say, after that Halloween, "Fearless Fly" was retired forever.

One of the nice things about being at School 18 is that each year I get to relive the magic of Halloween through the long tradition of the Halloween Parade. Seeing all the tykes dressed up in their costumes will serve as a reminder to me of a few essential truths. First of all, we need to preserve some sense of magic and wonder for kids. We have clouded their minds and robbed them of a chance to believe that childhood should last beyond the age of five: Our adult produced movies, games and conversations reek of material way too graphic for the eyes and ears of the wee folk. So, at 12:45 on Friday, I will not begrudge our students twenty minutes or so of pure fantasy. As much as I might want to take another try at that flying thing, I'll keep my two feet planted on Hoosick Street. Happy Halloween to all!!!!!!!!!!!!!!!!

November 3, 2008

The United States has been a flawed Union since day one. One of the premises that the founding fathers expounded was that, "all men are created equal". A grand statement but one not totally put into practice. I think these men, with their educated pedigrees, completely missed answering the big questions. How could they have thought that they were creating a democracy when so many human beings were literally held in bondage as slaves? Some of the biggest slave owners were the first career politicians. White men of privilege controlled just about everything. Native Americans were looked upon as obstacles to expanding the territory and so they were, for all intents and purposes, driven to extinction. Isn't it interesting that we wave the little red, white and blue flags every chance we get and yet pretend that we are the sacred guardians of a history based on the concept of democracy for all people?

Tomorrow, hopefully, we will participate in the practice of casting our votes for those who aspire to public service. Unfortunately, if past practice holds true, a vast majority of eligible voters will simply stay home. Apathy seems like a national disease. It has been a long haul since our independence from England was declared so many years ago. The Union was almost destroyed by civil war, women struggled to be able to cast a ballot and the descendents of slaves sacrificed their lives for the right to enter a voting booth. After all of the struggle, after all the bloodshed it still doesn't sink in.

The key to a successful democracy lies in the willingness of citizens to take the process seriously. One of the essential questions to ask is this, "What does it mean to participate in a democracy?" It seems to me that we have this fundamental obligation to search out the truth for ourselves. In this particular national campaign we have been bombarded with half-truths, mind insulting rumors and innuendos. What has been presented as fact often turns out to be pure fiction. The profession of journalism has deteriorated in some quarters to a slugfest among babbling idiots. The fact that some people take in this rubbish as absolute truth is most frightening. Being an informed citizen today takes work. It means reading, listening, absorbing, separating, searching. Basically, it involves cultivating the essential skill of thinking. Elevating thinking to its proper place is where our jobs as educators come to take center stage.

Classrooms need to be places where learners are allowed to question what they read and are encouraged to dig deeper and deeper. Like skilled cave explorers they follow the truth to the source while often traversing unsteady ground. Too often we have relied on textbooks that only told half truths or glossed over the untidy parts of our heritage. It is patriotism shielded from the horrors of history that lurked beneath the surface giving everything a spit polished look.

From whatever your political perspective tomorrow is a very important day. You will of course do some important tasks. However, perhaps the most important task of all will be to show up at the polling place and cast an informed vote. A vote based on the understanding that to participate in this democratic process, however flawed, is an essential obligation of living in this country.

It is our hope and the hope of all who will come after us that as a country we will learn from our past mistakes. The intentions of Jefferson, Madison and Lincoln were all most admirable. They gave us a foundation, however shaky. It is up to us to put the mortar in the cracks to insure that the house never crumbles.

November 10, 2008

It is clear from the state of the old maple tree outside my office window that nature is preparing for the long winter ahead. The branches closest to the windows are completely barren. All of the outer branches are trying desperately to cling to the last vestiges of faded leaves about to descend onto the soft carpet below. On this clear, crisp day the remaining leaves possess a golden glow that tells me that they have no interest in surrendering to the cold winds of December.

The stillness, the bareness, gives us time to slow down and contemplate our existence. As we have recently turned the clocks back, maybe we need to wind ourselves down and set aside some time to take stock of where we stand. November, a transitional month, bequeaths us the gift of time for reflection. It is a good time to learn from nature.

The Native Americans were probably the finest students of the ways of nature. They were taught as little children to actually study the wind, trees, stars and water. Textbooks were not consulted and instead these enlightened people passed the truths of life on to their children and grandchildren via story and ritual. I just finished an outstanding book, <u>I Heard the Owl Call My Name</u> by Margaret Craven that illuminates in a beautiful and stunningly simple way, the lessons the life cycle has to teach us. The story proves that sometimes you need to find your way through the eyes of a totally different culture. Acceptance is one of those qualities that often elude us. We would all do well to stop and think about how we can weave this teaching into the fabric of our everyday lives.

All cultures have their own unique voice to contribute to our stories. In each of our memory banks there are vignettes that need to be shared so that we can fulfill one of the tenets of our national identity. Ideally, it would have been nice if we tried to learn as much as we could about all cultures instead of choosing to dismiss some as irrelevant. In other words, we need to broaden our circle of understanding. The best

way to understand a culture is to seek out members of that culture and to interact with them in some way. For example, as a young teacher I was immersed, for the first time, in the African-American culture in the south end of Albany. Literature can also serve as a window of understanding for us. Both fiction and non-fiction can guide us as we search out the truth. Sometimes books serve as a springboard to more intense explorations.

Before we are totally engrossed in the preparations for the upcoming seasonal festivities perhaps we would do well to think about our own journeys. As the season of Thanksgiving is fast approaching it might be worthwhile to think about those people who have helped to shape our destinies. In more ways than one November is the perfect month to cultivate the practice of gratitude.

I will begin by being grateful for those leaves outside my office. They provided me with a cool breeze in spring and summer. As I watch them fall I will be conscious of the fact that nature indeed provides us with profound life lessons. It is up to us to take the time to look inside ourselves for the answers.

November 24, 2008

When I think of a culture that truly represents the finest qualities of natural born teachers, I always think of the Native Americans. As the holiday of Thanksgiving approaches this week I want to share with you a little wisdom from a favorite book of mine by Joseph Bruchac and Jonathan London, *Thirteen Moons on Turtle's Back*. In addition to wonderful text the illustrations by Thomas Locker are simply spectacular.

One of the pieces that I find especially relevant comes from a tale of the twelfth moon, (Lakota Sioux), "Moon When Wolves Run Together". The last paragraph goes, "So, in this moon, we climb the hills, lift our eyes toward the Wolf Trail and remember that our lives and songs are stronger when we are together". Forget the food, forget the football games and especially forget the temptation to take a road trip to Wal-Mart. The beautiful holiday of Thanksgiving is simply about coming together to share in a bond of connectedness. It is a day that symbolizes one of the best things the lawmakers of this country ever did. They made Thanksgiving a national tradition in 1789. Thus a day of gratitude was born. In most quarters it is a day that we haven't managed to destroy by wrapping it in a cloak of commercialization.

We gather from near and far with the people who comprise our own sacred circles to acknowledge that indeed, we are stronger together. It is a time to give thanks for the gift of life and for the opportunity to share this journey with the family and friends who serve as our earthly guides. In this day and age of constant disconnect it is so important that we set aside quality time to partake of the wisdom that members of our circles can impart to us. The elders of our clans can enrich our lives with tales relating to their vast experience of walking on this life journey. We all would be wise to give these elders the respect and awe that the Native Americans modeled so well.

In this culture we have come to idolize those people with ultra independent streaks when the simple truth is that we need each other. It sometimes sounds good to wish for a trip to a deserted island but in reality most of us wouldn't even survive a day of that fantasy. The idea of the lone explorer as a symbol of the g r e a t American spirit is mostly a myth. The truth of the matter is that this country was settled by bands of people who depended upon each other for their very survival. In fact, the country would not have been

able to survive at all save for the great generosity of the native clans who populated the northern coastal areas.

This coming Thursday we will gather around our tables of plenty and celebrate the gift of community. We will have much gratitude for the good fortune to be surrounded by loved ones. It would also be a great thing if we could take a moment to go outside on this day of gratitude and to simply observe the wonder of the natural world around us. One look into the star studded sky will remind us that we are but a speck, a tiny blip sharing our earthly journey with all that encircles us. Just like our native brothers and sisters we can celebrate our good fortune at simply being able to exist.

I wish for you this Thanksgiving the comfort of a warm fire, the laughter of family and friends and the knowledge that you are connected to all the seasons, all the cycles of the earth. Your heritage is the gift of those thirteen moons on the turtle's back. Hold it, cherish it and most of all, pass it on to those who will follow in your footsteps. If we all can remember to practice gratitude for the gifts that come across our path on a daily basis then the promise of the legacy of those simple souls who walked the hills and valleys of this continent so long ago will not be broken. Happy Thanksgiving!!!!!!!!!!!!!!!!

December 1, 2008

Well, I can say with certainty that the insanity part of the 2008 Holiday Season has officially begun. I woke up on Thursday morning to read the paper which, I might say, had twice as many retail ads bulging out from the center as it contained actual news sections. The huge ad sections are really nothing new but the time that "Black Friday" commences is particularly shocking this year. Shopping officially begins at 4:00am!

It is hard to equate Thanksgiving Day with the ultimate of family occasions when, if you work in retail, you probably have to retire for the evening at, by the latest, 9:00pm in order to be up at 3:00am or earlier to be at your post at the mega stores when the gates are opened at 4:00am. So maybe to accommodate the stores we should cancel calling it Thanksgiving dinner and push it back to Thanksgiving lunch. Macy's could perhaps be convinced to hold a midnight parade just so everything could be scheduled in and everyone could be in bed by 8:30pm on Thanksgiving.

Unfortunately, I think Thanksgiving really has gotten robbed of its significance to make way for the big retail event of Christmas. Actually, the madness begins in late August. The back to school sales are gearing up by July 4th before I have had a single day off for summer vacation. Halloween décor slips onto the shelves by early August and ever so cunningly, the retail giants manage to place some Christmas items in the stacks right after Labor Day. They give a nod to our National Holiday with a few turkey themed items but you can easily tell where the real stars of the show are. Before you turn the calendar to November, Christmas mania is in full swing. It is not only the stores that have been swept up in the nonsense. Home owners have jumped on board too. Several houses in my neighborhood have been ablaze with light-up figures, trees and other assorted neon stuff for well over two weeks. I am not a "return to the good old days" whiner but I have to admit things are totally out of control. If everything blends together, what is significant? Could we maybe just keep the Holiday piece behind the curtains until the turkey leftovers have been consumed? Can we wait for maybe December 1? Alright, I can comprise for the Saturday after Thanksgiving! Have we really come to worship greed as our true national value? What message does this send to our children?

I really love the beginning of the month of December and definitely look forward to the Holiday season. In my own good time I will make my way out to shop for gifts that will hopefully be meaningful to the recipients. I'll take some time to write cards to friends I don't get to see everyday. There will be a few parties to attend and maybe some lazy, snowy afternoons to sit by a fire sipping hot chocolate while reading Dicken's classic *A Christmas Carol*.

There is one thing I surely will not participate in. I will not be found exiting my garage on Black Friday morning before the night has even contemplated yielding to the daylight. There is no way I will line up in the cold with a herd of shoppers hoping to purchase what will amount to a needle in a haystack. No, I will probably spend my free time walking my dog around a quiet neighborhood. Hopefully, we will not encounter cars careening toward the mall for their chase. I prefer to think that my neighbors will still be snug in their beds, sleeping soundly after visiting with family and friends and talking well into the night. Shopping can wait, thank you, we are dreaming of those wonderful Thanksgiving memories which we just created. The Holidays will come soon enough and it is our task to savor each moment of this month ahead. You and I both know that before long the stuff with the red hearts on everything will be appearing. In fact, it probably is in the stores, behind the curtains, waiting for its way too early debut!!

Just as an aside on this December 1st, I would be remiss if I did not wish my nephew, Ryan P. Kilgallon, a very Happy Birthday. It was on a dark, cold December day 15 years ago that I made my way to Albany Medical Center with my mom to await the arrival of this little guy. He was supposed to be born November

10, but being the smarty that he has turned out to be, he chose to stay safely ensconced inside his mom for as long as he could. As my luck would have it, he was not in any hurry and I made my way back to work, leaving my mom to sit with her anxious son, Ryan's dad, Kevin. At approximately 11:00am that morning I received a call that Ryan had made his debut. As of today, fifteen years have flown by in what seems like an instant. That little golden haired lad is fast becoming a young man. He has made by life much richer by his presence. In this world of uncertainty and chaos I hope he makes good choices and enjoys a long, happy life. Most of all, I hope he comes to understand the gift of family and friends. Gifts that can never be purchased, no matter how early they open the stores. Happy Birthday, Ry!!!!!!!!!!!!!!!!

December 8, 2008

December is in full swing and to paraphrase Charlie Brown, "I know I am supposed to be happy." Holiday decorations abound, the shopping cycle is in full swing and the making merry stuff seems to be creeping into every aspect of life. The trouble is that this year it is taking a little extra effort to get in the Holiday spirit. The last straw for me was the unbelievable tragedy that took place at the Valley Stream, NY Wal-Mart where a man was trampled to death by shoppers on Black Friday.

It is my understanding that the items that these people came to purchase were electronic in nature, namely television sets. Not infant formula, bread, milk or any other essential item needed for the continuation of life. No, a man was killed because of raw greed and stupidity on the part of ordinary people and a mega corporation. Now let us all make merry and celebrate the pursuit of happiness gone completely out of control. Does anyone care to know what we have become as a society of allegedly decent, civilized human beings? What about this happiness thing anyway? How would you define it at the beginning of this season of peace and joy?

A great spiritual teacher once encouraged us to become like little children. I sat down to think about how I could best define and capture the spirit of that elusive quality of happiness. It has been said that the Buddha once held a gathering where he just stared at a flower. One monk "got it" and began to smile. I am beginning to think that happiness must be found in the simple values unique to childhood.

There is a wonderful musical, "You're a Good Man Charlie Brown". In the song from that show, "Happiness", the Peanuts gang has some pretty sound advice on the topic. Charlie Brown claims happiness is, "two kinds of ice cream", while his pal Linus says it is, "tying your shoe for the very first time". The pianist Schroeder proclaims happiness is, "catching a fire fly and setting him free". Perhaps the most important

advice comes when the whole chorus sings that happiness is, "singing together when day is through and happiness is those who sing with you".

Maybe it takes these characters of Charles Schulz's brilliant imagination to hammer home an extremely important point to those of us entering the 2008 Holiday season. Perhaps we should all put away our wallets and get out the song books. All of our cultures have within their histories some absolutely beautiful Holiday music. The songs are distinctly magical and capture the true meaning of this season.

None of these songs speak of the importance of material gifts or of anything even remotely connected with money. Rather they allude to the intangible delights of peace and goodwill. Maybe this year we need a song fest instead of a spend fest. Like little children singing their hearts out it won't matter how we sound. It could simply be a gesture to heal our out of control world. At this point in December, 2008 if each of us could sing a song to heal this weary world what a great gift that would be. Music, like the beauty of a single flower, has the power to do that. Maybe happiness is just a melody away.

December 15, 2008

As December shifts into high gear I always think it is helpful to stay centered in what is really important in life. The many distractions that are presented to us often leave little room for the gifts of quiet and reflection that we need to cultivate. One of my very favorite things to do every December to reflect on the meaning of this season is to read Chris Van Allsburg's classic, *The Polar Express*. Yes, it is a children's book but in my mind so much wisdom is found on the pages of this genre that I often seek solace there. Chris Van Allsburg is a master at weaving together interesting stories and beautiful illustrations with lessons of great moral value.

Each time I read this book I am grateful for being able to become reacquainted with the timeless quali-

ties of belief and trust. The main character is completely trusting as he boards the train headed for the North Pole. His belief in the magic power of the bell is unwavering even as he grows into old age. In other words, he has blind faith. What does it mean in this time of cynicism and disbelief to simply have complete faith that things will work out exactly as they are supposed to? Not how we want them to work out but how the universe has destined that they will. That, indeed, is something most people could use to work on, yours truly included!

Think back a few moments to your childhood at this time of year. In most traditions this is the ultimate time of wonder and awe. Before it is snatched away by the hands of time, the belief in Santa Claus is truly magical. Scores of children totally believe that a man in a red suit with a white beard flies through the sky on the evening of December 24 and somehow gets into the house, deposits all kinds of presents, sits down and partakes of countless plates of cookies and milk and then flies off into the sky in a sleigh led by a team of reindeer.

It is kind of comforting to know that in this time of "grow up as fast as you can", we can still hold on to the fantasies of childhood. All too soon the not really pleasant realities of growing up will make the waters rather difficult to navigate on many occasions. We will take on the burdens of the world and forget that we all need to parachute out of the escape hatch at some points in our life journey. Frankly, I think we need to stretch out childhood for as long as we can.

Not the self-centered, totally dependent, whiny part. What I consider precious beyond words is the starlight that appears in the eyes of those wee folk when surprise completely overtakes them and their innocence becomes as refreshing as a soft spring rain.

On this day that marks the midpoint in the month of December I find myself lost in a dream. A train whistle bellows outside my window sounding just like the ones I remember hearing as a child from the D&H rail yards. I float down the stairs and climb aboard. Surrounded by all of the friends and family from years past I sip hot chocolate and munch on my favorite cookies from Nelligan's bakery in downtown Troy. They were big white cookies with pastel dots on top. We speed away toward an enchanted land where only those that hear the bells can dwell.

Can't we go back there for one more day? I can't help but think that it would greatly enhance our collective mental health if we all just stopped for a few moments this 15th day of December. Try to bring to the forefront of your mind something that brings you genuine joy and peace of mind. If we could do this as adults this day just maybe we could ensure that the wonder and the awe could live on. There might not be a better gift we could give each other this year. So, pick up a bell today. Can you still hear it?????? Do you still BELIEVE??????????

December 22, 2008

This is the season when gifts of all types abound. Every where you go there are packages containing anything and everything imaginable from tiny boxes to gigantic stockings filled with a variety of assorted goods. Stores beckon, sales happen 'round the clock and the mall parking lots are filled to capacity. It is indeed a time of plenty. Of course the plenty is of the material variety. Why is it that when we think of gifts we generally think of the material kind? I can't help but wonder that this December might be a good time to refocus. Last weekend's terrible ice storm was a great example of what is possible when the human race is forced to confront the basic reality of life. The only thing that really matters is that our loved ones are safe. Did you notice that even strangers seemed to have a more caring spirit last weekend as opposed to the week before? There was a collective sense, for the most part, of "we're all in this together and we will make the best of it". It is too bad that it takes a crisis to light that spark in humanity.

I can't help but wonder what would happen if we made a course correction to the gift giving tradition of the Holidays. Instead of exchanging wrapped packages maybe we need to think about giving the gift of peace and goodwill to those around us. If each person literally made a concerted effort to be a kinder, gentler, less judgmental individual, then just maybe the potential of the human race could be realized. In the true spirit of every tradition I know of I truly believe we can all evolve to a higher state. Doesn't it all come down to the power of kindness to crack open some stone cold hearts?

There is a wonderful scene in the story, "A Charlie Brown Christmas" by Charles Schulz where Charlie Brown goes out to find a Christmas tree for the play and brings back a sorry little twig of a thing. The Peanuts gang laughs heartily at Charlie's folly and the tree ends up on a snow bank. Linus, the true believer from the pumpkin patch caper, retrieves the discarded tree from its' resting place. Sacrificing his trusty blanket to act as a stand he props up the little tree and with words of kindness, manages to convert the sprig into a thing of great beauty. Little Linus, great believer, loyal friend, reflective thinker and philosopher, gifted teacher, model of the power of kindness. Every time I watch the movie version that scene totally moves me. I think of the possibilities that abound if we could all just see how our words and actions can change the course of life. Try wrapping that thought up and gifting it to everyone you encounter in this season of hope and light.

A long time ago in a land far away from here a star guided some travelers on their way to witness a special birth. It was an event that promised to change the course of a rather disturbed time in history. Maybe we could use the light of the hope of this season to do the same thing. Each of us, weary travelers ourselves, can be witness to a re-kindling of the promise of the event we will commemorate at midnight this Wednesday. It can start when we make a solemn pledge to do things a little differently in the New Year.

My wish for you this Holiday Season is that you commit to rekindling the gift of kindness in your hearts. It is, however, a gift you should not keep to yourself. Just like that bright star that guided people to the birth of a new hope, allow the light of kindness to shine wherever you go. If we all did that each and everyday our power would never go out. Happy Holidays and best wishes for a restful school break.

January 5, 2009

In what surely seems like the blink of an eye, the year 2009 is upon us. The magic, and stress of the Holiday Season has left us and we are now confronting the possibilities that the New Year bequeaths us. A favorite quote from the sage of Concord, Ralph Waldo Emerson seems to offer some guidance in this regard. He states, "To be yourself in a world constantly trying to make you something else is the greatest accomplishment." If we all sat down to ponder this wisdom, I am sure we might find more than a grain of truth here.

How often in our lives do we give in to the pressure to be what society may define as a success? Do we go along just to fit in? I think this all starts in childhood and I am afraid that as educators we hold some of the blame. Our system is really set up to insure conformity more than anything else. In essence, we are sometimes threatened by learners or colleagues that show qualities a little bit askew from the norm. As the years go by, I feel the guilt of not cultivating my own uniqueness, but also of not doing more for those people in education who have crossed my path with different styles and ways of engaging learners. It has become a sobering reality to understand that difference is to be celebrated, not hidden behind a curtain of shame. Do we do enough in classrooms to reach the "outsiders"? Unfortunately, I think the answer is no. I am beginning to think that the business of "schooling" may be doing more harm than good. Why do we fail to honor dissent? Isn't democracy about listening, questioning, struggling with the hard concepts? Are we doing enough to create a culture that values everyone for their own self-discovered passions? Can schools really achieve the goal of turning out engaged, inquisitive learners who will dedicate their lives to finding out who they really are? Joseph Campbell put it so well when he encouraged people to "follow their bliss". Should we in this field settle for any less as we guide youngsters along the road to self-fulfillment?

I think of the few opportunities that formal education gave me to delve into those things that I might have wanted to explore. In fact, in my many years in the school paradigm, I do not seem to recall any. However, I absolutely love to learn but I now am beginning to question if the school system might have actually inhibited my education! I find myself questioning, as this New Year dawns, if maybe my future will involve a different path to help create a new school culture where learners can thrive. Frankly, I hear too much, "I hate school" from too many quarters and am feeling a responsibility to investigate why this is so in a country that spends an enormous amount of money in this area. For all the money spent, I think we fail to provide a meaningful experience for far too many kids.

Maybe it is time to give learners more say in what they may wish to explore. The idea of "teacher as guide" is hardly a new one but perhaps we should bring this concept to the table in earnest. A few decades ago I decided to investigate photography. I first observed people who owned 35mm cameras and then decided to purchase one after studying several different models. Since I was interested in learning the correct technique, I chose one that operated manually, as opposed to an automatic one that did all the brain work for you. Next, I picked up a copy of a Kodak manual and studied it voraciously. In fact, that book literally fell apart from use. I also spoke with people at the local camera stores who became trusted guides. Through trial and error, (mostly error), I became somewhat adept at the craft. I think I became a self-directed learner in the process. Also, it was something I definitely became passionate about. I now realize I must rekindle a creative spirit that I left behind when I put away my cameras many years ago.

As this year gives us an opportunity to create something that has literally never been before, think about your own life-long learning. Find your bliss if you have not already discovered it. If you have, do not neglect it. Like a good gardener, take care to get down on your knees and work the soil of your passions!! If we each gave each other the gift of encouragement think of how much happier we would all be. The freedom to be who you really are, despite the obstacles we will encounter, that is a legacy worth striving for. A life well lived is our destiny. Ralph Waldo Emerson knew this and we would all be wise to heed his teaching.

Best wishes for a New Year filled with the promise of becoming!

January 12, 2009

January has arrived and it is a hard month to get through, in my opinion. The weather seems to be bent on convincing us that winter is not interested in loosening its grip on us for several months. In my head I understand that living in the present moment is necessary for mental health but I just can't seem to help but wish that the 31 days of January were already behind us. February and March can bring their own horrors of the climatic variety but there is at least a flicker of hope that the thermometer will rise above freezing for more than a day. So, how then can we make January into a more tolerable month?

Perhaps January can be the month that encourages us to experience the wonderful quality of joy. According to Webster's dictionary, joy is defined as, "emotion evoked by well-being, success or good fortune-the expression of delight or a state of bliss". How often these days do you experience a state of bliss? It just takes about 5 minutes of watching the daily news to squelch any sense of bliss these days. Maybe instead of being <u>consumers</u> of the gloom and doom we should try to be <u>producers</u> of joy. If each individual took it upon themselves to bring even a little bit of joy into the world each day think of how everything would change. All too often we think of joy in reference to the big events of life like weddings, the birth of a child, graduations, etc. No doubt these events bring much joy to life but it is often a long stretch in between these occasions. In case anybody did not notice, our time on this earth is really not that long. I am beginning to think that part of our daily task is to share some joy. In fact, I think this is absolutely necessary work.

We are often under the delusion that what we do is more important than who we are. Our bloated egos look for verification that our jobs define us. In reality, the roles we play at work each day, while important, mask our true selves. The organizations in which we spend a great deal of our adult lives sometimes force us to be less than our best. Our real talents and gifts may never be known to our colleagues. In other words, too often work becomes a joyless enterprise. This is a sad feature of our culture. Work, devoid of joy is simply drudgery. Too many times organizations, in their quest for greatness, forget that creating that sense of bliss is one of the responsibilities they must attend to.

As I think of ways to increase joy I am reminded of a little scene I witnessed last year in a supermarket close to my home. It was a day in late January, gloomy and gray. That slushy ice that tracks everywhere was glazing the market floor. Standing near the check-out was a middle aged man of slight build holding on to a small planter filled with bright yellow daffodils. You could not help but feel joy at the sight of those flowers. The really interesting thing is that I was in the same store maybe a week later and I spotted the same man near the flower section choosing a planter filled with purple hyacinths. Clearly, here was a person who was conscious of bringing joy into his home in the darkness of winter. How wonderful to be evolved enough to honor the importance of creating joy!

Let us make a promise to each other as January inches along. May we bring light into the cold days of this month by finding something to be joyful about. Not necessarily something that will move mountains; simple is beautiful. Don't keep those joyful things to yourself but share them with someone here. A smile, a kind word or deed, they all count. I am not sure of many things in this often complicated life. However, just as February will over power the bleakness of January, I am sure that we can bring joy to this life. Without it we will all be less than we can be.

January 26, 2009

The harshness of this winter has provided my brain with plenty of fodder. I have no notion as to the reason but lately, my mind has kicked into reverse and I find myself reminiscing about the days of yore. They were by no means always golden days but they did have a certain consistency and rhythm to them. In the end I suppose history will be the final judge as to the merits of the baby boomer generation. So what follows is simply a little stroll down memory lane on a very cold late January day. Do you remember when.......

You got the news on a little machine called a transistor radio. Most of us owned the ones that only drew in the AM frequency. These were items that were generally received as birthday or Christmas gifts and ran on a single 9 volt battery. That was as high tech as it got. TV's were mostly black and white and if you wanted to clear up the "snow" that often dotted the screen you invested in something called rabbit ears. These were basically two little poles that formed a variation on the letter "V". Most of the televisions sold around here came from a company named RCA. They were made in the USA and if you were from these parts you took great pride in knowing that the RCA "dog" called "Nipper" sat atop the building in

Menands and stood watch over the whole Capital District. The well- to- do people living in Loudonville had their television sets enclosed in wooden cabinets with big speakers on each end.

We knew nothing of walk-in showers with gilded gold doors and ceramic tile floors. Actually, we took what was known as a bath and we did not have a cornucopia of scented products from a specialty bath products store to slather our bodies with. I recall we had a box of soap crystals called "Mr. Bubbles" that probably cost around 50 cents and was purchased to last over a month. Our towels were not color coor-dinated velvety plush things the size of bed sheets but were made of plain old terry cloth. Nobody ever counted the number of threads in a sheet.

A coffee pot was actually a pot that went on the stove, not a machine that sat on the counter top. It was generally aluminum with a percolator thing on top that looked like a glass fuse. The innards consisted of a skinny tube attached to a basket and it had no filter. Your coffee selec-tion was limited to two or three brands and no flavors. It was simply a coffee pot, it made a couple of cups of coffee—period. No way did it take up half the counter

space, program itself from two cities away or allow you to enter the kitchen to the tune of ocean waves hitting the beach in Fort Lauderdale. You didn't need an advanced degree in physics to operate it or take out a loan to buy it!

Back then people did not use the local emergency room as a doctor's office. You did not have ER frequent flyer passes and there were only three reasons for a trip there. One, you were bleeding uncontrollably and required stitches. Two, you stopped breathing. Three, you broke a bone which required a cast. Otherwise, you waited your turn in a general practioner's office. Band-aids and some orange stuff that stung when applied generally did the trick. If you cut your knee play-ing outside you went in, washed off the cut, endured a dab of the orange stuff, slapped on a Band-aid and went back about your business. No tears, no coddling and especially no drama. These things were not looked at as an "event".

Our family did grocery shopping at a store called the Grand Union – every two weeks you stocked up on the basics and maybe you could purchase six loose cans of soda if you were good. The 36 can pack of soda did not exist and no one I knew of would ever be allowed to consume that much soda in a year. Our childhood drink was a glass of lemonade made from 6 oz frozen cans (6 for a $1.00), which when diluted with water made a quart of liquid. We did not dispose of or recycle the pitcher because it was expected that it would last forever! Water came out of a tap which was not filtered or otherwise purified before it was consumed and we all lived as a result of drinking it. If we wanted a specialty food item we went down to a store on 4th Street that sold meat products. I remember the sawdust all over the floor and we would chomp on a cold hot dog or a piece of American cheese that we were given by the men who worked behind the counter in blood stained aprons. I don't know anyone who contracted salmonella after a trip there.

My parents went out without us on many occasions and it did not cause us to have nervous breakdowns. They simply hired a babysitter for the evening and that was that. We listened to the sitter without argument and we did not have to be threatened with drastic consequences for refusing to go to bed when told. Our "treat" was a quart of Pepsi and a 32 oz bag of Wise potato chips. That spread would end up feeding the sitter and two kids. We did not order 24 cut pizzas, barrels of chicken wings or gallons of soda. It would never have occurred to us to eat the chips directly out of the bag. The chips were emptied into a wooden basket and we took turns placing our freshly washed hands in the basket. The soda was poured into glasses, one to a customer.

Speaking of eating, we actually engaged in an activity called dinner. We would we not think of eating anywhere but in the kitchen, at a table, set with plates and silverware. Napkins were not optional accessories but were used at all three meals, unfolded and placed on the lap. No speck of food was wasted and you were constantly reminded of the less fortunate in other countries as you stared down at the remaining peas on your plate.

You definitely knew who was the parent and who was the child and absolutely nothing in your little life was up for negotiation. If you received a good report card you got a pat on the head not a trip to Disney or a steak dinner at the Barnsider.

There was no need for a walk-in closet in your bedroom because you never owned enough clothes to fill it. Your clothes were folded and placed in dresser drawers. One winter jacket hung in the communal coat closet. Designers were people who worked in Paris or Hollywood and no one in their right mind would ever dream of wearing their clothing line.

Perhaps most astoundingly, the activity, or lack thereof, of your father's reproductive organs were never discussed, let alone the subjects of prime time television commercials. Also, streams referred to something you fished in not a description of a male urinary output problem. In our wildest dreams we were never to witness a commercial with two adults sitting in bathtubs holding hands overlooking a pastoral scene to advertise impending "performance". That kind of thinking was subject to at least 5 Hail Mary's, 4 Our Fathers and 3 Acts of Contrition as penance at the post confessional altar rail.

Well, I guess like the long, cold days of January, this piece is finally going to come to a close. Maybe it has at least served to jog some of your memories back a few decades or so. As ways to pass the time this month goes, it may not have been a bad exercise. As we slide into the month of February in less than a week I will celebrate the fact that winter is half over. I might just have to stalk the aisles of the local mega market in hope of finding some genuine Moon Pies. It could be a long search. Hopefully, when I emerge, some bright rays of sun will remind me that Spring will indeed come back this year.

February 2, 2009

As I have stated before, I remain a big fan of the comic strip, "Peanuts" written by the late Charles Schulz. Over the years I have greatly enjoyed both his humor and the profound lessons on life in general contained within each piece. One of my very favorites is a treatise on friendship involving the characters Snoopy and Woodstock. The little yellow bird, Woodstock, is throwing a New Year's party and invites his dear friend, the clever beagle, Snoopy. A few days after the party, Woodstock serves Snoopy with a bill for $6.00 for something Snoopy allegedly broke while attending the event. Of course, Snoopy is highly insulted and refuses to pay the bill. As in most squabbles between good friends, a chilly period then ensues. When the two finally agree to talk Woodstock lets Snoopy know that he invited him because he was his friend. He wanted to introduce him to a bird he had a sort of romantic interest in. What does Snoopy go and do? He takes over the conversation all night, putting Woodstock in the background. The $6.00 bill, states Woodstock, was because you, "broke my heart". Coming to his senses, Snoopy feels completely awful realizing how deeply he has hurt his loyal friend. Grabbing Woodstock he proclaims, "Don't you realize your heart is worth more than $6.00?"

Friendship is definitely one of the true gifts of our lives. Whole books have been penned about it and countless poems and essays, too. We would all be less without the comfort friendship provides in times of happiness and sadness. Indeed, life would be incredibly lonely without at least a few trusted friends to make the journey beside us. Distance is no barrier to good friendships. You probably have friends who would drop everything and travel across the country if you needed them. Time doesn't seem to be a factor either. Do you have friends who you only see maybe once or twice a year but when you meet it is like you talked everyday? It is just as if you picked up the conversation exactly where you left off and there is no awkwardness at all. I think that sort of describes enduring, deep friendships. When I want a metaphor for that kind of friendship I often think of a raging, brilliant fire burning brightly on a cold winter's night within the confines of a fireplace. The wood crackles and sparkles and it is just one of the most comforting of human experiences. After several long, slow burning hours, the wood settles down to create deep orange colored coals that glow ever so dimly but still emit a sense of warmth and light. True friendships are like that because you only need to throw on a few sticks of kindling to re-ignite a roaring blaze once more.

February ushers in the month where friendship and its mate, love, take center stage. It is fun to see the little heart symbols everywhere, as tacky as they sometimes can be when plastered literally everywhere. I think it is kind of neat to see the once a year appearance of the giant red coated cellophane heart shaped candy boxes appear on the shelves of stores. Receiving red roses on a bleak February day can't really be all that bad. Even in friendship and love we all need to take time out and put our words into real actions. It is often the "doing" part that trips us up. It is so easy to take friendship for granted. We mean well, we really do, but in our crazed, harried lives sometimes friendships are too often sacrificed. It has been said that we are lucky if at the end of our lives we have maybe two or three good friends. I believe very strongly that friendships of this kind need to be deeply cultivated.

As in most areas of life we all need resources to help us along our journey. Being a huge fan of the written word, I have a favorite book of poetry that always helps me to regain a sense of the importance of friendship. *Will You Be My Friend?* was written by James Kavanaugh in the early 1970's. I hope it is still in print and it is well worth trying to find. Like all Kavanagh's writings, it speaks powerfully and directly to the amazing gift of friendship. It will surely touch your heart. In this day when hearts are so easily broken we all need a reminder, just like Snoopy did, that friendship is one of those truly special things that cannot be replaced. We would do well to never put ourselves in a position where any friend of ours serves us with a bill for a broken heart!!!!!!!!!!!!!!!

February 9, 2009

This week we will celebrate the birthday of a special president. Abraham Lincoln has enjoyed a new resurgence in popularity due to the commemoration of the 200th anniversary of his birth. Also, our new president, Barack Obama, has cited Lincoln in his speeches over the course of the last year. I, too, am an admirer of Lincoln although I tend to connect with him in praise of his self-taught mind and his persistence on learning the law on his own. This man has much to teach us about the possibilities of the examined life.

We tend to want our national icons to be perfect creatures in every area of their lives. Abraham Lincoln was one of the most revered of presidents but he struggled his whole life with matters relating to ethical and moral behavior. Lincoln eventually would sign the Emancipation Proclamation and abhorred the practice of slavery but he was not exactly an abolitionist. He was not convinced that the races could live together. His concerns were primarily focused on preserving the Union at all costs and a bloody civil war was fought on Lincoln's watch.

Lincoln was a prolific reader and writer. He spent many evenings engrossed in a volume of deep philosophical significance. In addition to prose writing Lincoln was a fan of poetry, especially Byron. Unfortunately, his family situation was often not the happiest and burying his head in books was a distraction for him. Like Ralph Waldo Emerson, Lincoln's one true love died young and he probably married more for convenience sake than for romance.

As Doris Kearns Goodwin details in her excellent book, Team of Rivals, Lincoln was not afraid to assemble a cabinet of former rivals to help him govern the country at a very unstable time in our history. The similarities to events facing us in 2009 are uncanny. There is no doubt that Lincoln was a conflicted individual but he always endeavored to live an honorable life. He struggled and struggled to insure that his actions were true to the ideals set down by the revolutionaries who founded this country. That certainly was a difficult thing to accomplish due to the fact that the country was founded on a giant compromise on which actions did not match glorious phrases such as, "all men are created equal".

History does indeed provide us with examples of ordinary people who rise to accomplish extraordinary things in times of great stress. It is up to us to uncover our own history lessons. Textbooks have so often given us the "cleaned up" version of history. If we are to truly honor the foundation of this country, blemishes and all, then we must become detectives. With every piece of information we are presented with we must examine it up and down, sideways and from every angle imaginable. Our duty as citizens of this country is to question and explore the source of the information we are given as gospel truth.

The memory of great American leaders like Abraham Lincoln will only be kept alive if we take seriously the challenge they left us with to uncover the truth. Indeed, it is the only way we will have earned the right to call ourselves a free people. As educators we cannot leave this up to chance. The very foundation of our democracy rests on our ability to encourage all learners to become proficient readers and writers. This is the hope of the fragile bond that keeps these 50 states united. History has shown us what can happen if these bonds are torn apart by partisan squabbles. Abraham Lincoln lived, and died, in the hope that the civil war would never be repeated. We have the privilege of carrying on that legacy, of truly living the examined life.

February 23, 2009

I consider myself to be an accomplished observer of life. Ever since I was a tyke I took a rather peculiar liking to sitting back and just watching the sometimes strange happenings of the species labeled human beings. Why I did not end up in the field of anthropology might be a question worth pursuing at some point. But alas, it is the depth of winter in the great Northeast and this mind is hard at work trying to figure out the comings and goings that occur within the walls of the modern day invention better known as the supermarket. This place yields much fodder for a study of human behavior and would certainly answer as to why, frankly, we are a sort of messed up lot.

Grocery shopping is one of those tasks that usually just has to be done and most of us find ourselves, due to work constraints, leaving this bit of unpleasantness for the weekend. Much like doing seven loads of laundry continuously this task requires some mental gearing up so to speak. People tend to shop the way they drive. It would seem to me that going up the aisle on the right is the way to go but this logic is often ignored in the suburban mega market where I battle the crowds on Saturday afternoon. Cart driving is worth watching. I often wonder why carts are parked directly blocking a row of items so one inevitably has to ask for it to be moved or risk the ire of the shopper if you touch their cart. Since I do not like engaging in any conversations while grocery shopping, this is irksome. I think there should be a lane down the middle of the aisle for cart parking thus leaving the shelves clear.

Some people clearly have a cart arrangement system. They group similar items together and have a neatly stacked cart as they proceed to the check-out. Others just pile everything in the cart and wheel around the aisles with reckless abandon. I think their carts probably mirror their lives, harried and spinning out of control. Often they have a couple of kids dangling off the sides of the cart trying to sneak everything sugar laden and expensive into the basket.

The deli section is an interesting side show. I usually only visit there to get maybe a half pound of turkey but usually end up behind someone with at least five or six

items. White American cheese seems to be the big seller and customers seem to favor whatever turkey is on sale including the slimy stuff that only resembles the real thing in color. Even though we talk of the importance of good nutrition, shoppers seem bent on taking the easy way out. How anyone can eat roast beef that hardly looks like it saw the inside of an oven is way beyond me.

I think one of the hard parts about grocery shopping is that there are just two many varieties of items. Do we really need an entire aisle devoted to cereal? Of all the brands probably four may have anything nutritious worth swallowing. The same goes for the bread aisle. Now there is not just wheat but honey wheat, flax wheat, 7 grain, 9 grain and 12 grain. Oat this and fiber that, white, rye, dark rye, flat bread, wraps, rolls and every mish mash concoction you can think of. All this at a time when most of us could use to simply cut out the bread all together.

Like running a race, the best part of grocery shopping is seeing the finish line. This country is still the home of over kill as far as eating goes. Rarely do I see grocery bills under $100.00 these days. I think with the stress of daily life maybe we all feel the need to treat ourselves and food is the source of our pleasure. As winter runs what I hope will be its final laps, maybe this is a good time to stop and remember that in spite of the state of the country right now we still should be grateful. Even when people come zooming down the aisles driving the grocery carts like they were in the Indy 500 I will be thankful for the opportunity to have a job that allows me to join in this madness. After all, given slightly different circumstances, I could be standing in a soup kitchen line. As any good anthropologist will tell you, societies that fail to look out for each other are doomed to suffer a very bad fate.

As we close out this month of February, let us take a few minutes to think about our obligation as global citizens. Unfortunately, there are many among us whose carts are literally quite empty. If this economic crisis does not soon turn a corner we will see more people in dire straits. More citizens will be driven to make choices that they never dreamed that they would have to resort to,then grocery shopping will be the least of our worries.

March 2, 2009

Sometimes a book has the ability to grab you by the throat and make you stop right in your tracks. Reading such a treatise becomes like riding a bullet train where night and day go by like a complete blur. Before you know it the last page of your destination is upon you and you are left slightly dazed by the experience. *The Shack* by Wm. Paul Young is just such a book. It is hard to categorize this work. While it does have a religious theme the text is far more spiritual in nature and this becomes an important distinction. Due to the tragedy that marks the beginning of the book I had put off reading it and it sat among my "unread" volumes for several months. However, after the third person I met eagerly inquired if I had read it I picked it up last Saturday afternoon. By Sunday afternoon the last page was digested, and like all powerful stories have the ability to do, I was left thinking about how I would incorporate the lessons of this book into my everyday life.

Without divulging the plot let's just say that putting the teachings of the book into practice is not an easy task. It is, though, well worth the effort. Instead of professing to know the great truths what if each individual person just made it a priority to become a better person? Forgiveness might be a good place to start. Think of how many grudges we carry around that go back decades. Small, silly things get blown all out of proportion and then the clock runs out and one of the parties is no longer around. More time is spent on petty paranoia then is spent on constructive solution seeking. We are humans and therefore by our very nature we are imperfect. One of the keys to living an honorable life is to seek to be people who choose to see and celebrate the basic goodness in others. It is way too easy to judge, criticize and try to mold other people to our expectations.

The book does bring one front and center to acknowledge and confront the presence of evil in the world. It is a presence in our lives we simply cannot ignore. Unfortunately, humans are capable of the most heinous of acts, particularly against children. As educators I believe we have the ability to help the most damaged of souls. I purposely say help because tragically some of the children we encounter have already been through too much to ultimately be turned completely around. Our acts of kindness in the way we speak to them may allow us to crack their shell of mistrust. We have absolutely no way of knowing how much pain any individual we encounter may be in at a given time. I am appalled when I see disregard for even common courtesy among people who should know better. Words and actions are definitely within our control. The horrific tales from Columbine High School have proved what happens when alienation occurs. When children of this bent reach adulthood they often become perpetrators. In other words, abuse begets abuse.

There are many things in this life we simply, by design, will not understand. We are left with the choice to choose love or hate. Perhaps if we all could spend time in a secluded mountain shack confronting our own weaknesses we would emerge freed from the chains that bind us to our lesser selves. In the meantime the power of Wm. Paul Young's book can serve to anchor us in the understanding that in order to move forward we must go back and heal the wounds that keep us from practicing forgiveness.

March 9, 2009

I read an article recently that brought up an interesting hypothesis. Is the current economic collapse connected to a lack of virtue? I believe a strong case can be made to support this theory. The simple virtues we try to engender among our students, such as responsibility, honesty and an ability to think critically are at the root of this mess we find ourselves mired in.

How responsible were some bankers and other financial people when they encouraged unqualified buyers to attempt to purchase homes that there was no way they could afford? It makes no sense at all, when paperwork is required for every small transaction in this culture, that proof of financial stability was not required to take on a 30 year commitment. We need to follow a procedure that is really not that complicated. If you don't have the cash to buy something then you probably should not think of owning it. The credit thing has exploded way past the idea that the only two items one needed to delay payment on were homes and cars. Now everything from gasoline to pizza is paid with plastic. It is not surprising that kids do not know how to make change when all they see people deal with are plastic credit/debit cards. Actually, there was a time not too long ago when you took cash/coins to a bank and handed the teller an object known as a passbook. It was stamped in the deposit column. The object of course was to have more deposits than withdrawals. You received 3 or 4% interest on your money. In other words, saving money was something you aspired to do. It was, simply, your responsibility.

Some trusting souls lost their retirement savings because dishonest financial advisers were only out to enhance their own nest eggs. They literally lived lavish life styles while their customers were being swindled out of their life savings. What happened to being good stewards when it came to caring about something you were entrusted to guard? Unfortunately, this is not limited to the financial world. Dishonest contractors abound, often preying on trusting senior citizens. Politicians and other government officials lie and steal their way to the top only to crash to the ground in a heap of embarrassment and shame. It becomes difficult to separate fact from fiction and the virtue of honesty is, in some quarters, becoming scarce. Even the field of professional athletics has been tainted by the blatant lies told by those athletes often worshipped by children.

If there was ever a time when critical thinking skills need to be valued the time is now. How did we get in this spot? What can history teach us about how to intelligently figure this out? Does throwing enormous amounts of money at a problem help us to solve it?

Maybe, maybe not. Do we have the courage to come together as a diverse population to challenge the culture of greed that threatens to undo us?

As educators we have a special role in this dilemma. The lessons on character are just as important as those of academics. What good will come of an educated society devoid of ethical standards? A long time ago some very wise people predicted what could happen when a society chooses to chase after the cash cow! At our best we should be people who care about other's well being first-period. Those of us who have the privilege of working at School 18 can be proud of the fact that we have built a caring community. The best we can do is to continue to uphold the standard of caring.

Like any family we will have moments when we squabble and disagree. However, also like any good family we will wrap our blankets of caring around each other so that no one stays cold for long. At the end of the day we will have done our small part to uphold the virtues that will keep the next generation from having to repeat our mistakes. That, my friends, would be quite a contribution!

September 21, 2009

Last spring I got the idea that some form of stress reduction was in order. Since I really like being around water I investigated purchasing a small watercraft to use on weekends. After some deliberation I settled on a 12 ft. red thing constructed of fiberglass and better known simply as a kayak. Of course, when one attempts to learn this skill much more "gear" is needed than the boat. Armed with paddle, life preserver, etc. I ventured up into the hills of Grafton to a serene reservoir devoid of motor craft. Let us just say that getting there, in this case, is not half the fun. That is a whole other installment.

The first few times on the open water were spent experimenting with a new skill set and the use of muscles seldom called into action. Getting the hang of kayaking is not as easy as it may appear. Toting around an 80lb. hub of fiberglass presents its' own set of challenges. After a few missteps the craft was launched into a calm body of water surrounded by trees and the entire scene exuded peacefulness. The third adventure, however, would prove to be a tad more complicated.

All began well on this late August outing and I spent a beautiful couple of hours cruising along with the bright sun as my constant companion. That old saying, "quit while you are ahead" should have served as a guide but it is seldom adhered to in my world. After two hours in the blazing sun on a rather warm day paddling a kayak tends to tire one even if you become oblivious to the warning signs. Well, I should have known better but decided to take one last trip into a small channel under a bridge that led to a scene more reminiscent of the swamps of Georgia than the hills of Grafton. Trees and vines surround you on all sides and the narrow stream is just wide enough for a couple of kayaks to maneuver side by side. The prize is going in far enough twisting and turning to the point where several beaver dams appear. Along with the sounds of softly running crystal clear water you are sometimes treated to the sight of the furry woodcarvers themselves standing like sentinels along the shore.

The problem was that I realized as soon as I crossed into the channel that I was not up to the task of paddling all the way down the banks. At this point I decided to bail out and turn the kayak around to head back to shore. Turning a 12ft. kayak around in a very small space, I soon discovered, is not as simple as putting a car in reverse! The first time I tried the kayak refused to slow down and I slammed head-on into the opposite bank. With a crash I realized I had stranded myself on a rock. No problem, back up, and then get tangled in some overhanging vines-well done! Now the boat is horizontal to the shore line but I need it heading

straight ahead. I grab onto a low hanging tree branch to stop the whole process. Did you ever try to think straight when you are so tired you can hardly move your arms? It isn't pretty and I knew I was close to the edge of panic. What would I do if I had to spend the night secluded in this wilderness? The mind is a funny apparatus and I got a taste of the power of it that afternoon.

This story has a happy ending in that after five or six tries I was able to somehow turn the thing around; mainly because I had to. In my life many wonderful and interesting teachers have helped me navigate through some rough waters so to speak. Never in my wildest dreams, however, did I ever think that one of those teachers would appear in the form of 80lbs. of molded fiberglass. On that August Saturday afternoon I learned some very worthwhile lessons that we all might ponder as we sail away into this brand new school year. First, you are stronger than you think you are. You have been blessed to have inside your head a brain that, if you just tap into its' magical powers, can lead you to solve even the most complex of problems. Just make sure you exercise it every single day. Second, don't ever give up on yourself. Persistence pays off big time! Re-group, re-focus and forge ahead.

The most important thing I learned is that nature really holds all the cards as far as power goes. We are just little tiny beings next to nature's immense power. All of us would do well to take the time to meditate on that thought. Your ego is the last thing you should worry about building up. Awe of something other than our own greatness is really where the focus should be in this life. Those were a few of the lessons that I took away from the school at the reservoir that afternoon. I will look forward to the new school year that will begin in the spring of 2010 when the melting snows yield to days filled with the promise of spring in the hills of Grafton. Somehow, I don't think I will mind hauling those 80lbs. down into the water. I just don't want to be late for school!!

October 5, 2009

The concept of success is certainly an interesting one. Not only is it difficult to define, but it is subject to much speculation as to how to actually measure it. The measuring thing, I have come to conclude, has led us down the wrong path. As a matter of fact we have driven so far down the wrong road that it will be a long haul to get back on to the main highway.

Our version of success tends to focus on getting things. The biggest house, the most expensive cars, more degrees, the latest and the greatest of anything money can buy. Our self worth is often defined by status symbols that have little to do with living a life of meaning.

This hit me over the head last weekend when I received a phone call from a close friend. Her thirty two year old son died during the night from a violent seizure. Eammon was born perfectly formed but suffered the first of many traumatic seizures at the age of six months. The seizures would not so much affect his body but, like an unwelcome home intruder, they completely ransacked his mind. So how then do we, brainwashed by our success obsessed culture, measure the value of a well lived life such as the one of this young man? In other words, what are the lessons he left us to contemplate and hopefully implant into our hearts and minds? Mostly, these are lessons that belong in our hearts because too little attention is given to the fact that our hearts have turned stone cold and we could use the light of feeling to thaw them out a bit. In this life it will be the relationships we cultivate and not the stuff we accumulate that will lead us out of our collective abyss. My young friend Eammon's light shone so brightly that it was able to thaw even the most hardened of hearts. Devoid of the trappings of our quest for success he was able to experience something that often aludes us-pure joy.

It would behoove us to stop and reflect for a while on the true meaning of a successful life. What good does it do to "plow ahead" and climb to the top of the mountain if so that when you get to the summit the valley looks exactly the same from the top as it did from the bottom? The only difference is that you have ravaged the trail on the climb up. Kindness can't wait. Families and friendships need to be our main course not just the treats we consume after dinner.

This is the perfect time to re-kindle a formula for success. The pace slows down and just like the leaves that are slowly turning into their magnificent colors, we too, can turn ourselves outward. All of us can endeavor to spend more time working on our connection to those around us. Be people who refuse to forget that life is all too short and that we must stand for what is right and just. If you need a reason to believe just look at the faces of the young children that you interact with here at school each day. They look to us to be fair, to be kind and to be honest. These are the years that will help form them into the adults they will all too soon become.

Eammon's mother wrote a beautiful obituary. She captured the essence of this extraordinary soul when she stated, "he was all things, great and small." Yes, he was a model of how limitations can be conquered and lead to an ability to truly inspire. Eammon lived, in the finest sense of the word, a simple life. The beauty and dignity of that life is beyond words. But I am confident in saying that without a shred of doubt that his life could be defined as an enormous success. It is this kind of success that we would do well to hunger after. For after all is said and done, isn't this the only kind of success that really matters? I will never forget Eammon's wonderful smile. His light will burn brightly to light my path, this I am sure of. Safe travels my gentle friend, safe travels!!

December 21, 2009

Today marks the Winter Solstice. Perhaps this is the day we should make the big deal about in December. It often seems that the other December headlines have fallen victim to the jaws of gross commercialization. More shopping, more consumption has become the mantra of this season. All that really comes of this is more anxiety and more stress. We are all cajoled into finding the perfect present then finding the right outfit to wear to attend the perfect party. So it goes until our bank accounts have the taken the perfect hit.

The solstice, on the other hand, could be a kind of simple reflective experience. No need to do anything but ponder the wonder of the season of stillness and quiet. The shortest period of light should give us pause to consider the gifts of darkness. What if we just lit a candle and gathered around our tables to enjoy the experience of being together? Every human face looks softer when it is reflected in nothing but candle glow. Sharing a meal by candle light can be a pretty nice experience on a chilly winter evening. It forces us to slow down to tune in a little bit more.

Why not put an end to the stress of the Holiday season by re-creating some new traditions that do not involve spending money or scurrying to every party we are invited to? Perhaps, then the true meaning of this beautiful season would gently come back to us.

Could it be that the first step toward healing our weary selves is to evaluate the need to drive ourselves crazy in the brief season of peace? Is exhaustion the purpose of it all?

The three phrases that I have underlined have become very important to me. In fact, I have them written down on a yellow Post-it note that I carry around in one of my pockets. They come from a wonderful book that was recommended to me recently, *The Magician's Elephant* by Kate DiCamillo. It is an inspiring tale, written for a young audience but like most of that genre, the wonderful metaphors are geared for adult understanding. As a gift to yourself this season pick up a copy and carve out some quiet time to read it. This book will not disappoint you. The illustrations are beautiful in their simplicity and the message, as I found out, can have a profound affect on the way one chooses to live one's life.

The strength of this book lies in the assumption that anything is possible if we will only believe. Too often we use regret as a guiding star when the secret to living a great life is to use the light of the present moment to guide the way. As the wise spiritual teachers have all reminded us, all we really have is the present moment. It is up to us to live those present moments with integrity and joy. We owe it to the world to be sincere, caring beings who truly believe in the magic and the wonder of each day.

On this day of winter solstice 2009, I gift to you the space to ask yourself three little questions. How do these questions fit into your own life right now? Perhaps you could implant them on your brain as you go through the hectic days to come. Maybe they will become a mantra of sorts as you try to stay centered and focused on those things in your life that are really important.

What if? Could it be? Why not? So, by whatever light you sit around tonight on this shortest day I wish you the peace of quiet contemplation. What if everyone could just stop and make a promise to treat people and animals and the planet with a little more kindness? Could it be that one decision like that could put the world on a better path? Why not?

Please accept my heart felt wishes for the happiest of Holiday Seasons. May the year 2010 bring you closer to achieving your hopes and dreams.

January 4, 2010

A new year a new decade has dawned and with it comes the promise of new days to shape into meaningful experiences. A quote from the Bhagavad-Gita comes to mind, "For the uncontrolled there is no wisdom, For the uncontrolled no concentration. For the unconcentrated no peace. For the unpeaceful no happiness can be." If ever great knowledge was contained in a tiny grain this statement personifies it. We would be wise to study this ancient text because it gives us a window through which to view true wisdom that is useful as we navigate the early moments of this new decade.

This new blank slate of time might be a good opportunity to cultivate a sense of calm. Maybe that is what this world needs more than anything else, people who can just be calm. It seems that on some level we have a collective case of the jitters. As everyone knows, it is impossible to live a quality life when you are constantly wound up and ready to pounce at every perceived slight. Of course the sounds that accompany just about everything electronic today can impede even the best effort to remain centered. Couple that with the constant need some people have to invade even the airspace with private conversations and you come to understand the challenge. As far as conversations go, perhaps we all could use to turn it down a notch. Did you ever notice that some people have an insatiable need to chatter, whether in person or on email? That kind of empty rhetoric is both annoying and plain boring. It simply contributes to the crisis of noise pollution and is mostly a way for insecure beings to avoid confronting skeletons in the closet. Circuits that are always full with nonsense cannot possibly hear the voice of rationality that demands a quiet pathway to be heard. Those that practice Zen meditation intrinsically know this. We do not have to be Zen masters however, to partake of the gifts that silence bestows to those willing to empty their minds of clutter.

Think of the consequences that have resulted from a simple lack of control. Self-discipline has gotten a bad rap lately. The result is an obsession with instant gratification in all realms of life. Obesity is running amuck because our nation is hard pressed to put the brakes on self-control. Food is used to solve all kinds of psychological issues and this only masks our collective unhappiness. It is just symptomatic of a culture spiraling way beyond the boundaries of sanity. We gorge ourselves, we covet food like addicts, we don't exercise and then we have the nerve to complain about health care costs!

If you drive a car you can easily understand the problem. I observe that red lights have replaced yellow lights as the caution signal. The times I have seen people race through red lights are too numerous to mention. We talk, we text, we drink, we push the accelerator down and in doing so we gamble with other people's lives. Are we becoming incapable of controlling anything anymore? We have to have the last word, the last cookie, and we don't seem to give a hoot about crushing somebody else to get anything we want in the least amount of time possible.

Is it any wonder that a sense of true peace remains out of our grasp? We are overweight, over stressed but basically under lived! I think a life well lived is akin to a nice leisurely drive in the slow lane. The final destination is not always planned and you take the time to park the car and just sit awhile to enjoy the gift of just being alive. Did you ever notice how cats are drawn to a sunny window in winter time? If you want to know about the whole concept of peacefulness follow a cat around on a sunny day in January. Little Zen masters, these tiny creatures are, just stretched out absorbing every ray of window filtered sunshine that comes their way. I had the honor of studying under the tutelage of a fine Siamese cat named Alex who lived to be eighteen years old. He lived this long, I am convinced, because he understood that slowing down was an essential component of a well lived life. No human voice could disturb his concentration and in this meditative state

Alex always appeared blissful. Sometimes our "happiness teachers" can be found in the strangest places!

On these long, cold January days maybe bliss is as close as sun beams filtering through windows covered with ice crystals. Wisdom, concentration, happiness, all those qualities spoken about in the text of the Bhagavad-Gita might just be as close as a blanket placed on the floor in a sun drenched room in the depths of a winter day. Here's hoping that we can slow down long enough to take advantage of this special time!!!!!!!!!!

January 11, 2010

Beverly Beckham, a writer for the Boston Globe, had a recent article published in last Sunday's Times Union. It was titled, "Resolve to do what you love". If ever there was a piece of sage advice applicable to us as we enter this brand new decade this article is it.

The story centers on a 94 year old New York City woman by the name of Carmen Herrera. She has been painting for over 60 years but she only recently has become a "star" of the art world with her paintings bought and placed in famous museums. In addition, her work has garnered rave reviews from the New York Times. The bottom line here is that for all these years Carmen Herrera simply chose something she loved to do and went about it with complete passion. She really never cared if she sold one single painting stating, "I do it because I have to do it; it's a compulsion that also gives me pleasure." This statement reflects back to what the late mythologist Joseph Campbell implored us to do when he said, "FOLLOW YOUR BLISS."

Sometimes the bliss will involve our actual work life and sometimes it will have no connection whatever with our day jobs. Unfortunately though, in this perfection obsessed culture, we have a hard time just doing something for the simple reason that we just really enjoy doing it. Basically, I think we are people pleasers and our egos get smack in the way of trying out new things just for the simple joy of experiencing something different. We need not be the most accomplished, most successful, or the most brilliant at our chosen activity. All we need to do is to have the courage to step off the plank into uncharted waters.

Maybe we would all become more contented, a little more joyful if we studied people like Carmen Herrera. Ask yourself what music is still inside you. What is your bliss and have you followed it or just day dreamed about it? Do the people you work with here know what really brings you joy? Would our world be a different place if everyone followed their bliss? Happiness alludes us because we do not believe we are important enough to take the time to express our true inner selves. When we ignore our passions we deny not only our own well being but we deny the world a chance to experience our best selves. Isn't the process just as important as the product?

The Carmen Herrera lesson is a good one. It is nice to be recognized for something that you are passionate about even if you have to wait nine decades for it! However, recognition has absolutely no relationship to happiness. If you wait around to be validated for your passionate undertakings you might just need to live to ninety years old!!

One of the few good things about this long, cold month of January is that it affords us plenty of time for reflection. Maybe that reflection will give us the time to compose that song, write that poem, prepare to run that marathon, bake the perfect cake or paint the scene of your dreams. Just don't wait too long. The odds that you will live to see 94 might be a long shot!

So…..as they say, there's no time like the present.

January 25, 2010

For some reason I have been thinking lately about the concept of simplicity. As much as I don't like the month of January it certainly helps cultivate a thinking about when the stark landscape and blowing snow encourages a mindset of semi-hibernation.

One of the loveliest conceptions of the concept of simplicity is contained in the words of the song "Simple Gifts". This song has rich history and was written in 1848 by a Shaker elder named Joseph Brackett who resided in Maine. Although the song has been used and re-arranged on many occasions, as recently as in Barack Obama's inauguration, it is actually a one verse dance song. So, even a simple song can be made into something so much more complicated than it started out to be.

"'Tis the gift to be simple, 'tis the gift to be free, 'Tis the gift to come down where we ought to be." It all just kind of makes sense, in theory anyhow. The Shakers were absolute models of simplicity. Studying their culture gives us insight into how less can actually be more. Just look at the design of their buildings or gaze at the lines of a piece of Shaker furniture. They are striking in the beauty of simple functionality. Perhaps what hits one on entering a Shaker building is the elegance of a space devoid of clutter. There is a remarkable connection between freedom and simplicity. However, it seems that our culture does everything in its' power to encourage us to become good pack rats. The "stuff" we manage to accumulate is truly unbelievable. It should be asked as to what purpose does it all serve? How many sets of dishes do we need, how many outfits, books, whatever! Think for example of all the clothes you have but seem to only wear a tiny fraction of them consistently. We just have our old reliable favorites and what is wrong with that?

Perhaps this is indeed the time to "come down where we ought to be" and resolve to think and act differently. One simple gift we can give each other is the ability to allow each person to be exactly who they are. That means no judgements or editorializing on style of dress, way of speech, or how someone chooses to live their life without harming anyone else. If we ran our legs the way we often run our mouths this country would surely be awash in athletic prowess!

I have long been a fan of the paintings of the artist Will Moses probably because I find them incredibly simplistic in the finest sense of the word. One of my favorites, "Travelers Moon", depicts a winter scene where people are coming and going from a roadside inn. As I sit here on a January evening, I take comfort in staring at the depiction of a full moon, a snowy countryside and friends gathering beside an old-fashioned fireplace. Somehow, someway maybe we need to re-connect with the simple values that are pre-programmed deep inside our brains.

In the end I'm not sure I could live the Shaker lifestyle. I am too much of an individualist to exist in communal living on a daily basis. However, I think I could certainly live without half the stuff I have acquired over the past several decades. Maybe true freedom is as close as the local Dumpster. Sometimes, in order to walk toward something you must simply walk away from something else.

June 21, 2010

I love the month of June for many reasons. It is the official gateway to the all too brief season of summer. In our business it signals the completion of a ten month journey with all the ups and downs of being part of a learning community. It is a time to celebrate the many accomplishments and also a time to sit in quiet contemplation and acknowledge the failures, the missteps that have plagued the year. Finally, June to me is a hopeful time. In spite of the things that didn't go so well, there is something rejuvenating about biting into a just picked, locally grown strawberry or gazing into the petals of a red geranium. As the humidity creeps up and the body slows down the eyes seem to gravitate to the brilliant burst of colors that separate this season from the shades of gray that dominate the winter landscape.

This week we will put the 2009-10 school year on the shelf. We'll close the books on it, for better or worse and move on. The ability to move on is certainly a gift that life offers us. Standing still for too long doesn't really do anyone any good. In that spirit of moving on I offer a few reflections on our journey this year.

As individuals you have proved your dedication to the field of teaching. I have witnessed your ability to stretch the minds of our young learners by putting forth both great effort and great patience. You have been builders, counselors, healers and magicians. I continue to be amazed by your willingness, day after day, to simply believe in your students even when their little quirks drive you to the outer edges of sanity. Frankly, I stand in awe of your energy and talents. What you do so strikingly well is something I can only admire from the sidelines.

This year for some reason I noticed an increasing gap in our ability to truly embrace each other in our differences and to make those differences into an affirming community. For this failing, I take full responsibility. As brilliant as we might be as individuals we have not reached the place where we can honor and celebrate our differences without judgment. If we cannot get past this, then ever so slowly, we will get caught in an undertow that will cause us to self-destruct. It is not about agreeing all the time, it is being willing to see things from a different lens than the one you usually look out of.

In the years I have been here I have tried to honor the wide range of personalities that I find in this nest. As I reflect back on this year I think one of my biggest failures is that I tried to be all things to all of you and that is nothing but a recipe for disaster. Actually, when you go down that road you end up just losing your core and that serves no one. In some ways I look in the mirror and don't really like what I see there. So this summer I will take my own advice. I'll try to find a spot under a big shady tree and, kind of like the Buddha, I will just sit and try to heal both body and mind. In a year of literal and metaphoric loss the climb back up will be difficult but it must be attempted anyway; even if the climb involves moving on. Some answers cannot be found in books.

Finally, I want to say good bye to some very special people who have enriched my life by their very presence here. Sue B. has defined the word grace for me. She has been an exceptional first grade teacher and her quiet dignity continues to inspire me. What an unbelievable foundation she has given to these beginning learners over the years!

Joy S. has showed me that wonder is a necessary quality for a well lived life. She has made art into a journey of self-discovery for so many of our children. I celebrate your "out of the box" style Joy. You give me courage to follow a different path.

Sue P. and I met at School 2 many moons ago. Among the gifts that she has given me perhaps the greatest is her ability to be my course correction compass. When I have veered off the highway onto the wrong exit, Sue has, not too gently, pushed me back on course. For this and for being the best bulletin board engineer I know, she will always have a special place in my heart.

I have known Ginny O. for what seems like a life time. We grew up on the same street and I have always thought she was one of the smartest people I ever knew. In addition, as I watched her care for the blind lady who lived downstairs from me years ago, I came to understand what the word compassion meant because that was what high school student Virginia showed to Helen. Your life has been a model of excellence and your quiet strength has never wavered.

Nina M. has been a life line in so many ways. Another friend from my early Troy days, Nina has shown me that hope is a quality I need to cultivate. Through times of great darkness she always lit a candle and carried on with dignity and style. Nina has been an outstanding ESL teacher and is a master of that genre. She is also an intellectual in the finest sense of that word and I know she will soon be found holding court in the Village in New York City. Nina has taught me the importance of place and until you find where it is you truly belong you will be less than. From Nina I learned the beauty of an Italian heritage.

To all of you I wish the very best of summers. I am grateful for all the lessons I have learned from you this year, even the really hard ones. Sometimes you are rewarded when, after a gloomy, torrential storm you look up to see the most stunning rainbow.

So, I will go back to eating those strawberries, knowing that although they might not taste so sweet this year, they are a gift none the less.

June 28, 2010

The days of June are so precious. I love the month of June primarily because it serves as the gateway to the summer, the season of possibility. In fact, the full moon this past weekend with its bright, pinkish hues made my brain want to dwell for hours in the pool of the possible.

Coincidentally, or maybe not, I just finished a fabulous book by one of my favorite authors, Paulo Coelho. When I first gazed at the title, *By the River Piedra I Sat Down and Wept*, I hesitated to take it off the library shelf. Who needs a sad book to begin the summer reading marathon? Based on my satisfaction with Coelho's previous books I included this one in the selections for the day. It was a very good decision to do so. This book provides magnificent insights into the realm of the possible.

In the beginning pages Coelho writes, "Every day God gives us the sun-and also one moment in which we have the ability to change everything that makes us unhappy. If people pay attention to their everyday lives, they will discover that magic moment…a moment when the power of the stars becomes a part of us and enables us to perform miracles."

It seems to me that way too much energy is spent on unhappiness. We lament our inability to find the perfect job, the most beautiful home or the issue free partner. The winters are too cold, the summers too hot. Our children are not rocket scientists, beauty queens or Olympic hopefuls. We are too skinny, too fat, plagued with aches and pains. Our hair is too long, too short, too blond, black or gray. Time passes too quickly, time drags, growing up is good, growing up is bad. Did we choose the right car, coffee maker, shirt, suit or sock? Is the TV screen big enough? That kind of thinking, engendered by a culture intent on promoting a collaborative unease, leads us into pursuing the illusion that happiness is somehow just beyond our grasp, a little over the boundary line.

Paulo Coelho reminds us that we are provided with the tool to undo the malaise. The mind is the key to the magic of everyday life. Like everything else we are provided with, there is a right way and a wrong way to use the tool. We are, most of us, magicians capable to feats of astounding beauty and decency. However, in the race to covet all things material, the only thing we achieve is a grand sense of disillusionment.

Maybe all the wisdom we need is not locked away in the ancient spiritual texts. Certainly, those words can guide us to achieve a higher purpose. After all is said and done perhaps it is in the power of the stars to show us the path to true enlightenment. When you look up in the summer night sky and see the thousands of tiny specks of light you realize that you are part of something much greater than your earthly form. You share this miracle called life and that fact alone should bring even the weariest of beings a cause to celebrate the happiness of our birthright.

On these amazing summer nights I will endeavor to keep one simple fact in the forefront of my mind. The stars will fade away, the darkness will envelope our earthly home but it will yield to the light of a new day where, God willing, I can dwell in possibility. Happiness is just a thought away.

July 5, 2010

Some of us are highway people. Maybe not in the literal sense of the word but, on the other hand, the thought of the open road is never far from our minds. The type of individual I am talking about has the "I can't sit still for too long" mentality. In school where you were forced into captivity, we were the ones most often found gazing out the windows watching the birds or the squirrels in nearby trees go about their daily routines. I, for one, envied their seemingly unscheduled life styles. According to their rule book the passage of time was not inscribed on the invention called the clock. Rather, existence was gauged by periods of great activity peppered with moments of, what appeared to me, contemplative stillness.

Highway people know that they should probably include themselves more often in the social milieu that buzzes around them and which provides a ready made source of non stop activity. Constant opportunity abounds for stimulation and the internet provides entrance to chat rooms 24/7 where conversations can tap into any conceivable subject. Highway people know they should tune in but almost always choose to tune out. Maybe the highway instinct is in our genes.

We are the quintessential gypsies, the seekers, the wanderers. Could we have been the old souls who jumped the trains, camped out under the stars or followed the pull of the moon toward the ocean where we walked along deserted beaches to the rhythm of the waves caressing the sand?

My own highway instinct goes way back to sun drenched early July mornings many moons ago. I remember waking up to the sound of songbirds and heading out to the garage to retrieve my bike. It was an old stingray type painted a blue gray with a bright white banana seat and for many glorious summers that bicycle was my own means to discover the gift of freedom.

I drove down the blacktop coated streets and flew up a small knoll into an area known as the sand banks. The narrow foot paths ran along a drop off beyond which there were large sand dunes interspersed with old trees. The sight from the path was stunning with an overview across the Hudson River and beyond. Unfortunately, the entire area today is home to a rather sprawling apartment complex.

Back in the 60's I would ditch my bike and walk softly among the tall grasses entwined with wild berry bushes which freely provided a succulent mid-morning snack. Deep blue sky, soft warm breeze and the rays of an early July sun provided all the stimulation I required. Grasshoppers bounded around and the hummingbirds warned of the need to seek out a shady tree for an afternoon siesta. I often wonder where a kid today could go to commune with nature unafraid, unburdened, free to simply enjoy the gift of a fine summer morning. I was not tethered to a cell phone and my ears were not invaded by headphones but rather my senses were completely open to the sounds and smells of a new day ripe with promise.

Today the highway calls in a different sort of way. I have been fortunate to have experienced many early July mornings all full of hope and promise. This year I might hunger for home but yet feel pull of the highway calling out to me. After all these years I still remain a restless spirit. Even now I gaze out my office window into the giant maple tree and watch the resident squirrels frolicking up and down the sturdy branches. Just beyond the grassy lawn Hoosick Street beckons travelers headed to Vermont on this Independence Day weekend.

The legs are again restless and even though the two wheeled bike has been replaced by a steel box with four wheels the call to wander remains exactly the same. There are just some imprints that even time cannot erase. I will always be grateful for a life time membership card to the highway club. Thank goodness that there are still some things that money cannot buy.

July 12, 2010

Summer is a good time to let go of some dietary rules. Most of the year I try to be some what conscious of the need to at least attempt to protect my heart among other organs. However, summer seems like a fine time to let loose a tad and enjoy the traditional picnic treats such as grilled burgers and hot dogs. Due to the fact that I am a self-confessed sugar addict I try to steer clear of daily runs to the local ice cream stand, without much success I might add. One of my all time favorite treats that I find myself craving during these dog days of summer is the plain old marshmallow. It would not be a stretch to say that I could handily down a half a bag of these morsels without a problem. Indeed, they are a sugar junkie's main line delight!

Sometimes I wonder how I would have done as a child subject in Walter Mischel's "marshmallow experiment" conducted in the 1960's at Stanford University. Basically, a child was placed in a room and one marshmallow was made available. If the child refrained from eating it for twenty minutes he/she was given a second one. Some children could not wait it out while some could. The researchers followed the subjects into adolescence and then drew some very interesting conclusions. Those children who were able to control the urge to eat the first marshmallow scored higher on the SAT test, had less problems with drugs and were generally better adjusted. It turns out that self control and the ability to defer gratification really are important qualities to cultivate, and not just among children.

The New York Times columnist David Brooks speaks to this very issue in a recent piece highlighting him in the " New York" magazine. Brooks discusses the Mischel experiment as it relates to the current state of affairs in America. His conclusion is that we are all gobbling the marshmallows. I could not agree more.

We are not only eating the marshmallows one at a time, we are stockpiling them at an alarming rate. One obvious example is the mess we have created in the credit industry. I can't remember the exact figure but the amount of debt held by individuals in this country is astonishing. The credit card companies are totally out of control and only government intervention will stop them from holding citizens hostage with the high interest rates on unpaid balances. The flip side is of course that we have no business buying most items we can't pay for. Our parents probably learned that lesson the hard way from their parents who lived through the Depression. As a result of a literal schooling in deferred gratification, that generation valued their savings bank passbooks more than their credit cards. Cash really is king and it is too bad that we threw that teaching to the wind, ate more marshmallows and continued on the path to financial ruin. Now it seems like too many people are eking out the minimum monthly payments on multiple credit cards in an attempt to pay for staples like food and gas that were consumed ions ago.

Starter homes are becoming ancient history. Why settle for a little two bedroom, one bath house when you can have a mini-mansion with four bedrooms, four bathrooms with glass enclosed walk in showers, kitchens with granite topped counters circling something called an island with enough room to seat a football team? Of course the view through the gleaming French doors showcases the sprawling plastic wood deck adorned with the fake lanterns called tiki torches. Let's not forget the mega stainless steel grill that can cook a Thanksgiving dinner in two hours. Last, but not least, we simply must have the eight person hot tub that drains electricity 24/7 in order to keep the water crystal clear and bubbling evenly at 100 degrees for that midnight weekend star gazing. All this so that the household of three can say for certain that they have achieved the American dream. What they have really achieved is a 30 year financed prison term of their own design with the big bank of their own choosing serving as the jail keeper. Can you remember having such things as US Savings Bonds that you kept for 25 years so you could put a big chunk of change down on a house? What is that song about America being the land of the free?

To top it all off we are raising a generation of kids who wouldn't give a second thought to grabbing the first marshmallow in sight. Please don't over tax them by asking them to read anything beyond a chapter a night. The majority of them don't read the classics but might be coerced into reading some science fiction or vampire tomes. Writing, more than a meager paragraph, forget about it! Give them instant-instant breakfast, micro waved everything else and let them follow their instant messages into oblivion.

This summer I am suggesting we return to an old ritual. How about if we all try a little experiment? Clear a pit in the back yard and using some twigs with crumbled up paper build a small campfire. Before proceeding to the next step just allow your eyes to feast on the incredible beauty of a crackling fire. Ever so slowly place a marshmallow on the end of a long stick and evenly roast it over the fire. Granted, it will take

some concentration and maybe a few tries but your patience will be rewarded. From deferring the urge to snatch the marshmallows out of the bag your taste buds will dance to the taste of the gooey white caramelized substance that will linger ever so briefly on the back of your tongue. Inhaling the smell of the roasted treats blended with the smoky air from the fire, you realize that summer is indeed a gift and an experience to savor. On this midsummer night may you sleep soundly dreaming of toasted marshmallows and slow burning campfires rimmed with tiny fireflies piercing a blackened sky.

July 19, 2010

This summer I tried something a little different as far as my work schedule goes. I took Mondays off thus giving me a taste of the three day weekend. Without hesitation I can say that I have become a total advocate of the idea and would highly recommend it as a means to a sane life. The extra day just seems to provide a safety valve with which to combat the stress of the weekend run around. No matter how hard I try, Sunday night arrives and I have not achieved anything resembling a recharged state of body and mind necessary to handle the challenges of a new week. The weekends carry an endless list of errands that appear to be shared by the majority of the population thus contributing to incessant crowding and lines that do not end. Even the local Starbuck's is inundated by 9:00am on a Saturday morning.

Last weekend, owing to the fact that I knew I had an extra day tacked on, I put off the car wash, grocery shopping, etc. until Monday morning. As a result of my very pleasant experiences, I am convinced that our collective health would improve if we chose the four day work week. It would be worth the extra hours worked on those four days just to be able to enter the supermarket without the feeling that one is about to prepare for a version of combat. At the car wash the $27 I spent actually felt like a worthwhile expenditure. It appeared that the inside of the car was cleaned instead of having the dust just moved around due to the constant stream of vehicles coming off the conveyor belt. In other words, the usual weekend grind of chores took on a positive mood altering tone.

It occurred to me that there is another benefit to having a bit more extra time. Perhaps we might be able to cultivate something that is sorely lacking in our hurry up, get out of my way culture. Just maybe, we might be able to think. It is clear, in my mind anyway, that the thinking piece could be the only way to salvage an attempt to live a respectable life. If the brain always has the fight or flight switch turned on then it denies us the ability to shift into the knowing gear. You can't run an engine at maximum speed with low octane fuel and expect it to last very long. History provides us with so many examples of the prophets of the art of thinking that all we need to do is set aside quality time in order to listen to their wisdom.

Aristotle, in his treatise *Metaphysics*, guides us to the simple truth that, "all human beings by nature desire to know". I think this gets to the heart of what it means to be an educated person. Sometimes it seems we have a propensity to define an educated person strictly in terms of credentials and degrees. There is surely something to be said for following the path lead-ing to the spoils of what is considered the normal route to attaining educational prowess. However, there is a place for the so called underground route also. The point is that quality thinking takes deliberation whether you are learning to diagnose an illness or learning to diagnose an engine failure. One of the linking factors in these endeavors is the ability to step back and to listen.

As July kicks into high gear I will take advantage of my remaining opportunities to enjoy a few more three day weekends. I am grateful to have those respites where time kind of stands still and I can just think. Unfortunately, unlike the sage of Concord, Ralph Waldo Emerson, I can't make a career out of thinking. I would however, on these sun drenched days of July, like to believe I can at least enjoy being some what of an amateur philosopher. I can venture out to find a quiet patch of earth. The only sounds I want to hear will be those of a gentle breeze whistling through the ripened green leaves that dress the sturdy forest trees. Chipmunks, ants and squirrels might share my little square of ground on this July morning. I will experience the great gift of life first hand and I will certainly have the desire to know how we have let the good life slip away from us so easily.

July 26, 2010

There is just something so special about a July day. This summer it seems the month has delivered everything that we wait for all year long. For the most part the rain has stayed on hiatus, the temperatures have climbed up into the 80's and 90's and the sunshine has been abundant. Maybe we have all been rewarded with an extra special gift from the universe for enduring the first half of a rather turbulent year. This has truly been a July to savor.

The other night I was driving home relishing a late July evening at about the time when daylight yields to dusk. The sun settles down and the heat of the day relinquishes itself over slowly to the gentle stirring of the evening breezes. Daylight winds down and the collective universe takes a deep breath before everything is ensconced in a blanket of darkness. I find this to be a magical time and it beckons one to be outside.

As I drove along Route 2 heading toward Troy I looked up into the sky and was treated to a wonderful sight. The full moon was rising up but it was hidden somewhat by what appeared to be a scalloped cloud of gray. It was as if someone reached up and pulled a shade down on it. Upon arriving home I again looked around to see whether the full moon was indeed deciding whether or not to grace the night sky. Through the cover of a group of trees the moon, tinged with a soft orange glow, lit up the sky with a brilliance I rarely get to see. To me, that brilliant, brightly shining full moon defines the potential every living creature has to make a contribution, a unique contribution; to this thing we call life.

Perhaps the problem is that we too often forget to pull up the shades every morning on our own full moons. We wake up looking at the day as a challenge instead of literally a once in a life time opportunity to shine brilliantly. Before we even get out the door we are burdening our skies with a list of tasks to perform, jobs to endure, stuff to purchase and goals to chase after. Many times all this leads to a sinking feeling that there are too few hours in a day to accomplish everything that we put on our plates. In reality, we are the guests of a perfect universe.

Summer is a great time to remind ourselves that life, lived consciously each day, can be a glorious adventure. We just have to take a little time to reconfigure the purpose of it all. The first step, in my mind, is to wake up with a mind set to stop all judging. In our human stupidity we think we are in control of almost everything we encounter. How many times do we wake up and one of our first judgments revolves around the weather? Doesn't it sort of go downhill from there? It might prove interesting to keep a running total of all the judgments we make in a given day.

Instead of all those external judgments, how about giving some thought to our internal motivations? Do we live each day with a purposeful passion for our work? If not, then the shade is pulled down over our true mission in this life. Collectively, we owe this universe our best. Because we are caught up with obtaining everything we think will make us happy we become less than and we lose our purpose, our center. It doesn't take a rocket scientist to figure out that we have made a big mess lately of just about everything.

On these waning July nights I will be found outside searching out that bright full moon. I'll be surrounded by the tiny night creatures singing their little hearts out. In the stillness of this late July night I will make a promise, one that I vow to keep in the coming months. I promise to live purposely, devoting more time to the things I am most passionate about even if it takes me in a new direction. I will make a conscious effort to do the work I came here to do. After all, although it is sometimes more comfortable with the shades drawn down, you can only shine brightly when you step fully into the light of your own design.

September 6, 2010

This is the time of year when there are tiny, subtle signs that change is in the wind. Looking around you can see that the leaves on some trees have actually begun their fall transformation as the gold, red and orange hues are gaining ground and are about to over take the vibrant greens. It is the life cycle reminding us again that the old must make way for the new. The season of fall once more proves to be an able teacher. This is a good time to follow the wisdom of the change of the seasons and to let some old patterns of thinking fall to the ground. Something is let go of so something different can appear. Fall is a season of hope.

In the spirit of a new season and a new school year I offer a few thoughts on a simple concept. The theory may be simple but the practice is what gives us trouble. How do you use the word? As history has so aptly proven, misuse of the word can have lethal consequences. Even today as the New York City mosque controversy polarizes the nation it becomes crystal clear that words can have a devastating effect on just about every facet of our lives.

I began thinking of this topic as I was reading an unbelievably wonderful book by Markus Zusak, *The Book Thief*. It is wonderful not because it is a happy book but because it showed how words can be used to enlighten, to move us for the good or, on the other hand, how words can be orchestrated to make us abuse or even kill our fellow human beings. Please consider reading this book as it has a life changing quality deep within it and the prose is superb.

I think we all have a fundamental responsibility to choose our words very carefully. They can literally change the course of someone's day and even the trajectory of their life. I clearly remember a chapter from my own past that had a profound effect on me. There was this nun who taught math at the grammar school I attended. From my childhood perspective she was just plain mean and her footsteps instilled fear in all of us. I have since, from an adult perspective, seen fit to forgive her for I realize she must have been a very unhappy person limited by her career choices. Anyway, she taught math but had no patience for those of us missing the mathematics gene. One day I was summoned to the blackboard with a few other students to solve a fraction problem. The others hastily figured out the answer and scooted back quickly to their seats. I remained at the board within several feet of "herself". Try as I might I could not figure out the answer and became more frozen by the minute. All I remember next is that the good sister went into a tailspin, her face becoming redder, the arms flailing and her body aimed directly at me. In the ensuing moments as I hit the blackboard I caught the word "dumb" being uttered as one of many adjectives she used to describe my ineptitude as a fraction problem solver. I surely redeemed myself in some way mathematically that year as I lived to tell the tale. However, that one word, "dumb", has followed me to this day as concerns anything mathematical. In other words, I became a math phobic and have since secured a life time membership in that society. Aversion to math of any kind has dogged me ever since that day and, unfortunately, I failed to understand that the deficiency was in the teacher, not in the student.

Today I try never to break the spirit of a child or an adult by the misuse of words. I know I will work on this skill forever as it takes a conscious effort to keep focused on being positive and not to add to the pain anyone may be feeling. We find ourselves in the midst of a word misuse frenzy these days. Talk radio has led the charge with speech that borders on hate being spoken by people who are basically peddling ignorance. The really sad thing is that so many people are blindly following these misguided souls into the abyss. Thinking through an issue before entangling oneself in a web of hurtful words needs to be a priority for all of us. As educators we must be vigilant as we can directly alter the course of a person's life by our use of the word in the school building. Children are indeed perceptive creatures.

Think of how history was plagued by the misuse of the word in 1939 Germany. People followed the word of one lunatic and the result was human destruction on a grand scale. The words of southern politicians in the 1950's and 60's led to unimaginable acts of hatred being perpetrated on innocent human beings due to the color of their skin. The list could go on and on. Let us vow to be people who, as Don Miguel Ruiz so beautifully states in this book, *The Four Agreements*, are "impeccable with our word." There is no greater gift we will give the children and our colleagues here at school.

As we ever so slowly begin the transition to a new season let us walk a new path. Encircled by the magnificence of the uniqueness of the season of fall in the Northeast, let us commit to maintaining the beauty of each person that will make the journey with us this year. If we can master this one skill, to be impeccable with our word, we will have given each other a gift as wonderful as the trees bursting with the colors that only nature can produce. May we all walk in harmony with that masterpiece in the days ahead.

September 13, 2010

The Eeyore character from the *Winnie the Pooh* books by A.A.Milne makes for a great case study. This fictional donkey, a childhood favorite for generations of youngsters and adults, too, is certainly an endearing figure. On the one hand he is a symbol of the stress free existence, sauntering along in the Hundred Acre Wood, surrounded by his other friends as they make their way through life. Unfortunately, the gray little creature represents all too well the glass half empty theory. He is gloom and doom, gray skies and the forecast of rain on a cloudless day. In other words, Eeyore is not what you would call a positive being. Like most of us, he could benefit from a little course correction from time to time.

I used to think that the positive thinking thing was just an extension of the self help movement. As time goes by, however, I believe that positive thinking is an essential skill for life in the 21st century. As Gandhi so aptly stated, "We must be the change we wish to see in the world." If we all made a concerted effort to be more positive perhaps the world would become a kinder, gentler place and wouldn't that just be the greatest thing! There is a tragic amount of pain in this world we inhabit, but like a master Aikido martial arts practitioner, we can cultivate the ability to deflect the painful blow instead of absorbing the brunt of it thus gravely injuring our psyche. Negativity is all around us but, so is beauty. It all comes down to how we choose to see the world. It is interesting to observe people in their daily comings and goings. Can you spot the Eeyores? They are good people but they have an ability to sort of darken a perfectly fine day with their predictions of the sky falling. You could be happy just to be alive but they will begin pontificating on anything from the weather to the state of the economy. You walk away with a little less spring in your step from just a one minute conversation.

There is no doubt that the Eeyore mentality has its' roots in family life. All parents want the best for their offspring. However, in the zeal to raise the perfect child we often forget that there will be a natural deviation from the mean which is really a very good thing. In each one of us there exists a spot where we innately know the path we wish to follow in this life. We have our own unique interests and curiosities. Too often, well meaning parents try to channel those interests into career paths that will not allow us to fulfill our true destinies. Childhood should be mainly a time of exploration and discovery. The nay saying and negative talk should be banished. When our kids come home with four A's and a C- what do we choose to focus on? Yes, Eeyore strikes again!

Schools continue the assault on our characters by striving for too much conformity. It is easier to teach to the center. The problem is that creativity is often found lurking on the fringes and it should not be cajoled into dwelling in the middle. As educators we need to be comfortable in celebrating difference even when it makes us a little uneasy. It is too tempting to view different through the lens of negativity. Very often we strive to fix something that is really not broken at all. Sometimes, as hard as it is, we need to refrain from offering sage advice and just act as a guide. The best guides are very familiar with the territory and can keep you from wandering off a cliff but they don't carry your pack up the mountain for you.

The coming days will definitely prove quite challenging. We will settle into a routine and the new beginning will become a distant memory. The glory and splendor of the fast approaching season of autumn will be accompanied by cooler temperatures and the realization that winter will be all too soon knocking at our doors. There will be the temptation to slip into an Eeyore attitude, looking toward the next day off, planning vacations and lamenting the beautiful summer that we just left behind. The only problem with all that is we fail to acknowledge the most important day of them all-today.

Eeyore is one lucky donkey. In the Hundred Acre Wood he dwells along side the bear with the weird name, Winnie the Pooh, eternal optimist. Pooh is also an extraordinary teacher. He sees the possibilities inherent in each new day. I believe him to be a bear of gratitude. So, here in our own forest and in the spirit of possibility, I will leave you with a simple thought. I wish you all a very happy Monday filled with all the joy your heart can hold. It is going to be a great day and I am grateful to be able to share part of it with you!

September 20, 2010

Most Friday nights due mainly to exhaustion, I sit home and watch a series of politically oriented news shows on public television. I greatly enjoy the discourse and their inherent objectivity. One of the shows this past week, however, hit me right between the eyes with a graphic display of violence from the fighting in Afghanistan. The savage brutality of war was front and center with the shooting of a young soldier as captured by an embedded news journalist. It is all such a waste and lately I am dwelling on a fundamental question. How do we take the war out of people?

It is not just the war waging on in distant lands. The rather frightening proposition is that war seems to be buried deep in the make up of all of us. Our weapons of mass destruction are the judgments we make about others without really thinking them through. We drop bombs of hatred laced speech out of sheer ignorance. Since we often will not take the time to really get to know people irrespective of the roles we play they are placed in a barbed wire fence that is impossible to climb out of. Instead of celebrating the good fortune of others we riddle their hopes and dreams with the bullets of disrespect.

Not too long ago we had the opportunity to listen to the very wise words of the educator extraordinaire Mary Montle Bacon. She spent several days trying to understand the culture of Troy and subsequently to help us move forward to improve the lives of all the students in our District. She left us with the charge to heal ourselves first by building a culture of trust, to break down the barriers that prevent us from doing our best work. In other words, she tried to take the war out of us. Like all master teachers Mary Bacon could only plant the seed. The individuals that make up this community must do the hard work of self reflection and then try to renew our commitment to each other. If we are going to raise the children right then our houses must be in some kind of good order. As of now I think the war still rages on.

So, on the dawn of a new season I offer a few suggestions to take the war out of us. I challenge you to add to this brief list and to continue the hard work so that hopefully, in the not too distant future, we will have brought a sense of peace here.

1. When someone offers you food, unless eating it will throw you into a diabetic coma, accept it. A while back, a totally evolved man by the name of Jesus was really into breaking bread and sharing it with all those around him.
2. Smile at someone and really mean it.

3. Get in the habit of going for a walk every day. Sitting and stewing about stuff never changes anything. Walking can become meditative and we could all stand to harbor less stress.

4. Stop using your car as a potential weapon. The horn is meant to be used in emergencies not to jolt a driver into moving faster than they should be.

5. The saying about money not being able to buy happiness is absolutely true.

6. Diversity, in the broadest sense of that word, is an unbelievably beautiful concept.

7. The only thing that can completely take you down is your own ego.

8. Cultivate the virtue of patience.

9. Plant lots and lots of flowers. No one ever walked out of a field of flowers without feeling a sense of wonder.

10. Spend some time with a dog to learn all about something called loyalty.

11. Make it a point to get to know a person you work with a little better. The talent here is unlimited.

12. Watch what comes out of your mouth. One stupid comment can literally ruin a person's day.

13. Learn to accept yourself, shadows and all. Striving for perfection only puts you on the wrong path.

14. Open your heart. Love is something to run to, not away from.

Finally, step outside on a clear night and gaze up at the stars. Then you will realize that your spirit is connected to everything in this universe; by yourself you are nothing. You came here to become part of a great chain, a mystery that you will never completely understand. If we are ever to honor the gift of walking on this earth we must all work very hard and make a promise to each other that we will take the war out of us.

September 27, 2010

This journey we call life is certainly interesting. Along the way, we are, I believe, provided with messages to guide us toward the truth. The messengers often must take strange paths to get their point across because the recipients can often be blockheads. In this respect I am implicating myself. So this is a tale about a flower, a card and a box. The moral of the story is that we must be people who listen carefully to the messages the universe is attempting desperately to send us and then to have the courage to act.

Many years ago I would often visit my grandmother's house on a regular basis. I loved going there because she was a happy person who always had a stash of M&Ms in a gold ceramic dish near the dining room window sill. During my frequent visits to that dish I would notice a group of plants neatly arranged on a tin cart directly under the window. They were little plants that were spectacular with their delicate flowers in shades of pink and purple. My grandmother was a master African violet gardener and I have always associated her with that flower.

Perhaps ten years or so I was given an end of the year gift by a student. It was, of all things, an African violet in a tiny orange plastic pot. A single light purple flower graced the plant. Since I possess absolutely zero green thumbs I just figured this plant would wither up and be tossed away. However, some nagging thought told me that I should at least try to water it once a week or so which I have done faithfully all these years. The problem is that for the vast majority of the time, all that appeared on the plant was a preponderance of green leaves with no sign what so ever of blossoms of any sort. I tried everything including an infusion of specialty violet soil but to no avail. Frankly, I was getting tired of looking at the sorry thing but try as I might, I just couldn't get rid of it. I suppose that in the recesses of my mind, it reminded me of my grandmother. So, now it gets a bit eerie.

Last year was not one of the easiest I lived through for a variety of reasons. Someone once said, "You don't know how strong you are until being strong is the only choice you have." So, needless to say, I looked for signs that things might just improve a little bit. Given that I tend toward the cynical side I really didn't expect much. One dreary morning I walked into the office and went over to water the always flowerless violet. Tucked underneath one of the leaves I noticed a tiny ball which a week later blossomed into the most striking, perfectly formed flower. Soon another appeared until four flowers erupted from the center of the plant. Since that time last year the plant has periodically produced gorgeous flowers from something that is root bound and really not well attended to. You can draw your own conclusions.

Recently I received a piece of mail with a note from a person whom I consider a wise guide. Enclosed in the note was a card with the words from Thomas Merton written on it.(*Thoughts in Solitude*) It contains some very powerful thoughts, including, "I have no idea where I am going. I do not see the road ahead of me." The point of it all is that sometimes you simply must just trust.

The third sign came in the form of a box. Actually, it wasn't the box or the contents at all but rather it was the conversation with the person bearing the box that carried the message. The conversation, however, probably never would have happened without the box. The messenger is a person of quiet strength, enormous intelligence and is one who does not live life surrounded by a cloud of fear. So the lesson from this person is as follows. You are not going to learn to swim by standing on the beach. The water might be cold and there are many times when you won't be able to see the bottom. But in order to call yourself a swimmer you have to swim. Just because you wear a bathing suit doesn't mean you could save yourself from drowning in a body of water. Granted, nobody ever drowned from lounging around the deck of a pool but few things compare to swimming in the open ocean.

These three people have something very profound in common. They are wisdom keepers. Each of them has presented me with gifts. The thing about gifts is that you must put them to good use. All the wisdom in the world is totally useless if it is not incorporated into the choices we make every day. The uncertainty of life is apparent and often it is not an easy ride. You could use a myriad of adjectives to describe all the bumps in the road. One thing will help us as we make our way. We must be people who recognize the sign posts that are literally every where. Close your mouth, open your eyes and ears. The sign posts may be easily recognizable or they will be as subtle as the early morning dew that appears on the grass as we slide ever so gently into the season of fall.

October 4, 2010

The air the last few mornings definitely carries the crispness that signals the season of fall is upon us. Early morning dog walks now require the addition of more than a light sweater and the maple trees are appearing a bit more barren. October is stepping up to bat reminding us that it will serve up some spectacular scenes of color but also that we will be walking along the gateway to winter sooner than we think. So October is a month where mixed feelings abound.

The October calendar tells us that the national holiday of Columbus Day is on the docket a week from today. It is the one holiday that I don't think we should celebrate and, in fact, I believe we need to completely eliminate it from the calendar. It is time to set the record straight about this so called hero. In a nutshell, what Christopher Columbus discovered was a group of peaceful people known as the Arawaks. Instead of trying to learn from their good nature he enslaved and slaughtered them. Columbus was simply a greedy mariner in search of gold and other riches. History can be so easily manipulated to further a false sense of nationalistic pride at the expense of innocent cultures. As educators, we have an obligation to tell the truth even when the rawness of that truth goes against the myths we have created and the lies we tell to make us feel a collective sense of absolution.

Lately, the attacks on the profession of education have reached a fever pitch. Outsiders, from politicians, business gurus and talk show hosts have jumped on the bandwagon to promulgate more myths in another attempt to further our nationalistic sense of accomplishment. So, again, the facts must be uncovered and the scare tactics finally put to rest. Half of these so called trends, like Columbus' search for gold, are just attempts to line the pockets of people who are willing to take advantage of innocent children. Every year someone comes up with another supposed solution to cure the ills of the national education disease.

Fire the teachers and administrators, discover everyone's unique learning style and teach to that each minute of the day, test until that is all you do and then pay teachers based on the student's scores and the ridiculous ideas go on and on. The only thing on fire in this country right now is sheer ignorance. What we need to demand of educators is that they step up, speak out and take back the profession before the hysterical cries of the "saviors" ruin us for good.

I am in total agreement with one voice of reason, the educational author Mike Schmoker. He wrote a great piece in the September 29, 2010 issue of "Education Week" on priorities. The foundation of good teaching is has to start with a solid curriculum that is used for all students. Schmoker then believes that students should, "read, write and discuss, in the analytic and argumentative modes, for hundreds of hours across the curriculum." Finally, he eschews the need for "good lessons". At the heart of the good lesson concept is the need to check for understanding. The most brilliantly conceived lesson will be a total failure if a student cannot understand the concept being taught. Maybe good, solid lesson design is where we should put the focus. This is where the art of teaching comes into play. The teacher's own intellectual creativity is of monumental importance. It is an enormous undertaking. One must be totally familiar with the curriculum, be able to analyze complex material and lead students to an understanding of it, practice critical thinking skills and hold student interest through good lesson building. Are we really ready to trust politicians, some of whom can't even grasp basic geography?

As educators maybe we need to stop playing the victim role a little and really step up. Complain less about the tiny injustices and begin to spend more time on the important things. Petty criticisms and faculty room gossip is wasted energy. The best way to support each other in this time of crisis is to help one another become better professionals. Interact, discuss and observe. We all have the capacity in this building to be mentors. Share books, ideas and articles. Talk about your lesson delivery with your colleagues.

What worked, what did not and why? Stretch your own intellect by tackling a piece of writing that you may find difficult. The brain needs as much exercise as the body. Most of all, don't believe that those outside the profession have the answers to "fix" us. All change comes from within.

We will manage to get through the coming week and before we know it the long weekend will be upon us. I suppose most people will still talk about 1492 and sailing on the ocean blue and all that jazz. This year I will see things a little differently. I am choosing to call October 11 Native American Day. I'll find a soft path in the woods to walk on, laced with leaves preparing to become part of the earth again. Walking in silence I will celebrate the culture of a people who understood that you do not need to seek treasure to fulfill your destiny. You just honor the gift of your life by taking care of your earthly home. These wise souls knew that they were given everything they needed for their journey. All they had to do was to maintain a connection. We would all do well to let that thought sail around in our heads for a while.

October 18, 2010

There was an event this past week that certainly signified the power of hope to stop the world in its tracks. The rescue of the Chilean miners may have been the break the weary world needed. Amidst the dreadful news of the economy, including the foreclosure crisis, hate crimes and nasty political rhetoric there was the power of hope in action. Hope that the human brain could engineer a rescue capsule that looked so simple yet was so complex and intricate that most of us could only imagine what it took to design it. Hope that 33 men could survive 69 days of a living hell beyond our ability to comprehend.

The same evening I watched an interview on television between a news anchor and the CEO of Capital Communications Federal Credit Union in Albany. Cap Com is one of the original sponsors of the "Making Strides for Breast Cancer" walk that is held every October in Washington Park. They have raised hundreds of thousands of dollars over the years and each year they seem to exceed the total raised the year before. The organization continues to hope for a cure and through their efforts the goal is getting closer. The CEO ended the conversation by adamantly declaring, "we'll be here until this is finished". Hope, commitment, perseverance all deeply engrained. In Chile and in Albany we see the power of thinking and acting outside of the self. A willingness to join forces and an understanding that when we work together there is no limit to what we can accomplish.

What ties these two events together is that they are great stories. They are cultural stories and thus define the culture of the organizations these people represent. The stories will give the members of these groups guidelines for how to act within the organizational culture. The miners defined what cooperation, faith and perseverance mean when they are acted out under extreme stress. The workers at Cap Com know that commitment and compassion are two fundamental, non negotiable goals within the organization which are spoken of and practiced from the top down. Violation of these embedded norms cannot be tolerated and organizational storytellers insure the continuation of the cultural history.

Story, then, becomes a powerful indicator of the health of any organization. In this time of global tension it might be worthwhile to make a collective pit stop to renew and recharge our spirits. In many cases we will need to literally try and call back our spirits due to the damage we have so often inflicted on each other by our words and actions. Each one of us brings her or his own individual story to the table and we need, as members of a larger organization, to take the time to listen to these stories. Each member must be acknowledged and valued for their unique untapped gifts and talents. Failure to do this leads to assumptions and judgments which can topple the best intended motives of any organization. Basically, I think we need to be people who excel at "taking care of". If we are ever to fix the ills that plague us we must set our differences aside and just become better care takers. Let our stories contain chapter after chapter of how well we took care of our earth, our co-workers, our families, friends, the creatures that we share the planet with and even our foes. The generations that will come after us need to read about how we were able to stop the great slide into the abyss because we set upon a new direction. That, because we saw the ability to care as our primary goal, we wrote a new story filled with hope. We dreamed of peace and that we would no longer tolerate acts of violence or hatred.

Here is something that I propose we do on one of these damp, chilly nights of October before we retreat to our dens for the long months of winter. We could all show up at a great campfire. All of us will sit in a circle as our native brothers and sisters showed us how to do when we are serious about honoring the spirits of one another. As we watch the bright orange flames shoot high up into the star studded sky and we listen to the dry burning wood crackle, we can begin to tell our stories. Maybe, if we do this right, we will ascend, just like the Chilean miners, ever so slowly from the darkness into the light of our own healing. Namaste my friends!

October 25, 2010

There is an exchange in one of the "Peanuts" comic strips written by Charles Schulz between the characters Franklin and Peppermint Patty. They are talking about test grades and Franklin tells Patty that he feels bad that she got a D-. Patty is really not fazed at all responding, "I'm just glad I have my health." We should all stop and consider that statement for a while. Health is something we take for granted until we lose it. It is also something we have a responsibility to maintain as best we can.

These days there seems to be resurgence in the interest in physical health. More people are exercising their bodies and working out in a variety of ways. Indeed, we seem to be experiencing a second "running boom" with races from the 5K to the marathon surging in popularity. Slowly, but surely, people are paying more attention to proper nutrition. We are heeding the message to eat more whole foods and to stop relying on less processed junk devoid of any nutritional value. So, there is hope that we are turning the physical health problems around. It is the mental fitness part that is causing us quite a challenge.

Every where you look you see ordinary people on the edge. We have become ill tempered, impatient and generally out of sorts. On too many days we trudge through with our only goal being to just survive the day. Too often the reward ends up being food or alcohol related which eventually leads to another set of problems. Unfortunately we come to resemble rats on a treadmill more than human beings enjoying a truly wonderful experience.

Actually, each day is really an invitation. Every day we are given a miraculous gift and all we really have to do is find our place in the sun, even on the most outwardly cloudy, rainy days. I'm not claiming that life is without upsets and genuine problems. Sometimes it can be very tragic. If we live long enough the sky will fall on some of our days. However, the glass half empty theory often takes the lead in the race of life. That is just plain too bad! There is a very appropriate quote from the musical "Mame" that is worth pondering on this last Monday in October. One of Mame's profound lines is, "life is a banquet and most sons of bitches are starving". What could life be like if we all decided to come to the table and feast on the banquet of life? It is really impossible to over stuff yourself on all the riches available at this table.

These final days of October offer up a grand opportunity to respond positively to the invitation life puts forth. Clean, crisp sunny days tinged with the scent of fireplace smoke are waiting for you. Who can resist the taste of a freshly baked apple pie washed down with a cold glass of apple cider? As close as Grafton Lakes or Saratoga State Park you can find a quiet trail to walk on and underneath your feet you can feel the crunch of newly dropped acorns. Who cannot be moved by the sight of little gremlins and goblins scurrying about in their costumes on Halloween night? Bright orange pumpkins abound in the fields by day and are transformed at night into glowing sentinels that beckon us to come inside and enjoy the warmth of a fireplace. We get to feel the comforting touch of a wool sweater and the cold chasing heat of socks encased on our feet. Mugs of hot chocolate will once again tickle our insides and remind us that there are still some pleasures to be enjoyed when the temperatures drop.

So, maybe this is the best time to answer life's invitation. I am reminded of the gang from "Peanuts". Can't you just picture Charlie Brown, Linus, Lucy, Sally, Peppermint Patty and the ever present Snoopy frolicking around in the scenes from "It's the Great Pumpkin Charlie Brown"? The invitation is extended to everyone. It simply states, "Come on out and play!!" We would be wise to RSVP on that one right away. Indeed, our collective health depends on it.

November 29, 2010

As November months go this one has not been too bad. So far we have avoided a significant snowfall and the temperatures have remained some what constant even though the wind seems to have found some extra strength lately. We have officially kicked off the Holiday season without, in my opinion, giving Thanksgiving its' rightful allegiance. This year marked the first year that the big chain Sears decided to remain open on Thanksgiving Day. We just can't stand the thought of a day of peaceful reflection devoid, for even 24 hours, of the need to search out another product that we definitely don't require. Collectively we hunt for bargains, camp out in the cold, to have bragging rights to securing the latest electronic gadget, always seeking, coveting. All we do is fall prey to a culture that wants us to stay dependent on the materialism that has driven us into a debt that is staggering to contemplate.

We have become like children in our desire to be noticed, acknowledged, accounted for. It is as if our sense of self is measured by the number of text messages we receive, the hits on our blogs, all affirming that we are the center of the universe, that our existence is noticed and desired. I cannot begin to tell you the times I have seen people text, tweet, blog or whatever during meetings and other gatherings when their complete focus should have been on the speaker. We think we are the ultimate multi-taskers when all we really have become is the masters of rude behavior.

The need to be noticed and noted has driven us to spend more than we save and to seek identification in the goods we possess. Narcissism, once reserved for the truly disturbed, has become a national past time. Everything "worth having" carries a name, a label, a scent or even a taste. The blog system allows us to advertise our likes, dislikes, minds and bodies until everything private becomes public and nothing about us is left to the imagination. We matter because we say so!

Take a look at people's cars. Someone invented these little white circle stickers that tell everyone where you have vacationed. It is bad enough when we have to advertise where we send our kids to college but do I really need to know that you were at Martha's Vineyard, the Outer Banks of North Carolina or Lake Placid? For that matter, it doesn't matter to me whether you ran 13.1 miles or 26.2. I am glad that your car climbed Mt. Washington but, frankly, I'm just thankful mine can climb Hoosick Street everyday. So why do we find it necessary to tell every one everything? Have we become, like little spoiled kids, so desperate for attention that we believe telling all is the way to get it?

Maybe we should use the beautiful month of December to think about what is really important to living a good life. If you step outside these cold mornings just before sunrise you will be stopped in your self absorbed tracks. First of all the silence is wonderful and it does not require a response. Gazing to the east I notice a deep pink band of light illuminated by sparkling stars. I am surrounded by several pine trees whose fragrance I greedily inhale as I walk softly on the frozen grass. Looking up into the sky I feel something that cannot be bought because how do you package wonder? I am totally disengaged from the need to justify my existence. All I simply feel is awe and I know that compared to this vastness I am nothing but a tiny speck of humanity. At this moment I only feel gratitude. If only I could maintain this feeling as the day progresses and I am drawn into the demands of the daily whirlwind that will ensue. How did life ever become so complicated? That is a question I can ask myself as November slips away yielding to the frantic days of December.

Perhaps we could all give ourselves an early Holiday present. We could promise to spend more time in quiet contemplation of the beauty of nature even as the snowflakes swirl around us and the cold December wind makes us don an extra layer of wool. The funny thing about this gift is that you will not be able to buy it no matter how willing you are to stand in line. It is one that you have to experience totally by yourself. Reading about it on a stranger's blog just won't capture it!

December 6, 2010

The "season" appears to be in full swing. Every year I look for a story that can take me away, ever so briefly, from the trappings that, unfortunately, have come to represent this splendid season. This season's gift appeared in the wonderful book by Robert Fulghum, *What on Earth Have I Done?*

This true story commences in the Canadian province of Alberta, near the South Saskatchewan River. It takes place in the time just following World War One and involves a very poor family struggling desperately to survive on this secluded prairie. The story is retold to Fulghum by a woman named Gussie who was eighty years old at the time of the telling. She recounts in vivid detail the starkness of that particular winter of her childhood when the only thing the family had to eat was boiled potatoes and turnips. They huddled together to keep from freezing. Their mother was ill and confined to bed.

As the Christmas holiday approached the children understood that there would be absolutely nothing to denote the occasion; no gifts, no tree, no tinsel. They were just grateful to be "alive, warm and have something to eat". As everyone gathered Christmas morning Gussie's father produced an item of wonder. He held in his hand the simple gift of one single orange that was to be shared among the children. Those children considered the arrival of the orange to be a miracle. For one thing, their meager abode was hours away from the nearest trading post. Their father refused, for the remainder of his life, to discuss the origin of the orange. Gussie, however, never forgot the gift that would stay in her memory bank for the remainder of her life as one of the best presents she ever received. She remembers biting into the orange and tasting something as sweet and as pure as honey. The simplicity of it is astounding. It was a gift of sacrifice for sure. Imagine in the year 2010 receiving an orange as your only gift!

The power of this story lies in a simple truth. Love trumps all. It is a willingness to make an unbearable situation just a tad better by providing even a small token of kindness. Who could believe that an orange, shared among many, could change how someone views life? This holiday season finds stores packed to the ceiling with gifts that it will take some people all year to pay for. Cameras, ipads, televisions and even jackets can run into hundreds of dollars to acquire. The sad thing is that we sometimes assume that these extravagant packages will just appear before our eyes. Too often we feel guilty when we cannot provide the perfect everything. We fly around like little wizards tapping into our wallets like they were magic wands that make dreams come true. When everything is extraordinary then how do you appreciate the beauty in the ordinary?

The point is the simple gifts of this season are found in the ordinary. A glowing menorah that lights up a December night, a little sack of Hanukah gelt, the smell of freshly baked home made cookies, colored lights wrapped around a freshly cut pine tree, the special ornament that carries your childhood memories all provide a richness that should give us all the meaning we need to appreciate this season.

The weary world certainly could stand to rejoice right about now. So, maybe, like the newly barren trees outside, we need to just stand still and con-

template how we wish to acknowledge this season of peace and good will toward all. If we really can be true to the spirit of the season and share those tidings of comfort and joy with friends and foes alike perhaps we stand a chance of ushering in a new decade filled with promise.

We don't have to look far for opportunities to put this holiday spirit into practice. Spend less time in the malls and more time with family and friends. Don't think you have to spend all day cooking and setting an elegant table. That is really not what we are all hungering for. What we desire, in this time of disconnect, is to simply be present with those we care about. The venue, doesn't matter. The menu, doesn't matter. The miracle, just like the miracle of the Christmas morning orange, will be in our ability to reconnect with the family and friends that may have drifted away in the past year. That is the only thing that really matters. I am not sure exactly who to attribute this saying to but it is one that I need to keep in the fore front of my mind. "Those things that matter most should never be at the mercy of those things that matter least".

December 13, 2010

There is a thought provoking article in the December 1st edition of "Education Week". It was written by high school English teacher Bob Barsanti and titled, "The Classroom is Not a Factory". Barsanti compares the current educational reform rage with the time he spent working on a factory assembly line during his college summer vacation. In assembly line work all you really need to care about is that, at the end of your shift, the product conforms to a pre-determined standard.

So, too, in education it doesn't take much creativity to follow a scripted lesson and it is easy when you only have to produce a number at the end of it all. In other words, the conveyor belt mentality doesn't require something called thinking. Now we hear that our productivity quota numbers will be posted on the company bulletin board for all to see and even our paycheck will be contingent on our factory assembly line success.

Not too far from here, on the banks of the Mohawk River in Cohoes, is the site of the former Harmony Mills textile works. The old mills have been converted to upscale rental lofts but parts of the original floors and windows actually remain. It is interesting to imagine these poor women struggling to get to work on time on bitter winter mornings. They had to climb several flights of winding stairs to arrive at their posts. There they spent endless hours hunched over sewing machines and I am sure they had quotas to meet at the end of the boring day. Maybe the only thing they looked forward to was a lunch break sandwich and a cup of hot coffee. I stood in one of those lofts several months ago and could picture these women spinning the cloth on machines spewing oil. The old wide plank flooring probably creaked and groaned while the wind howled creating bone chilling drafts blowing in from off the river. There was probably zero chance for what we would call creative work. Did we leave this scene behind in the 19th century or have we resurrected the concept of it in the name of reforming an educational system that those removed from the classroom think is broken? In the recesses of my mind I think about that saying warning us that history repeats itself when we do not heed certain lessons. Right now I can totally relate to Bob Barsanti's lament.

Think about those rare individuals you had as teachers over the years who really moved you. First of all, their energy and enthusiasm was contagious. They were so passionate about the subjects they taught that you hardly ever saw them sit behind a desk. Perhaps these individuals tended toward the eccentric side of the scale. Because of their unwavering belief in the students they were privileged to serve they set the standards of achievement very high. However, they also provided you with all the tools necessary to stretch your mind. The no limit philosophy was firmly ingrained in them and it was transferred to you. These gifted people were not necessarily easy on you, many times just the opposite was true. You were challenged and your intellect was given the top billing it deserved even in spite of your whining that the material was way too hard. Although a textbook may have been used, these enlightened beings often tossed it aside to enthrall you with stories that enriched your understanding of the subject matter. They would have been insulted to even think that teaching involved following a script. Indeed, they practiced teaching as a creative art and each day was a new adventure steeped in possibility.

As I walk the halls of School 18 I see that kind of teaching taking place. I am confident that, years from now, your students will think of you in a place reserved for the best teachers they ever encountered. It is your ability to get your students to think beyond a basic level that will make the ultimate difference. The essential questions are WHY? and SO WHAT? I would encourage you as this year moves along to continue to be seekers and explorers in your teaching. The only way to accomplish this is to be a seeker in your outside of school life!

It is my sincere hope that we do not resort to the teacher as mill worker model of teaching. Each little person has a unique talent that needs to be nurtured and they need to be able to follow the beat of their own drum. The last thing we need is for our students to ascend the staircases of schools turned into factories where they while away the hours turned into products devoid of all artistry.

December 20, 2010

Tomorrow at precisely 6:38 pm we will mark the Winter solstice. It does not come one minute too soon this year. For starters, I think the really cold weather came a month early probably due to it being in as much turmoil as the rest of us right now. Between the cold and the darkness it seems like we were bequeathed a double whammy and all we can do is wonder why we choose to live here. Since I believe we own our choices I guess I should move rapidly to another sentence.

On December 21 one of the gifts that will come into our lives will be the return of the light. When you stop to think of it, light is something we too often take for granted. If you have ever dabbled in photography you know the importance of light. Actually, the light is most striking from sunrise to around 9:00 am and then from about 4:00 pm to sunset. The mid-day light tends to render objects flat. If you notice a flower for example that has the light coming from behind it, you can see unbelievable detail in each petal. The best photographers in the world live to literally chase the light.

In the book, *The Winter Solstice*, author Ellen Jackson describes how the solstice has been noted throughout history. The return of light has been fundamentally important in just about every culture.

The Romans gave candles to their friends and also started the gift giving tradition. Northern European cultures built huge bonfires and some even tied fruit to evergreen tree branches. These customs served as reminders that although the winter was long and cold, summer would come again. The concepts of love and forgiveness were also stressed. This all goes to remind us just how important light is to our well being.

On this solstice eve I would ask you to consider a simple question. How will you use the light? In this life we are all given the opportunity to spread either light or darkness. That is the meaning of free will. On these dark winter mornings we have the ability to light our internal candles and keep them burning well into the night. Those candles can glow with the flame of forgiveness, good cheer and peace. Unfortunately, they can also be easily snuffed out with thoughts of bitterness, anger, jealousy and greed. In this time of worldwide chaos and strife we all need to put in extra effort to keep our candles burning brightly. More than ever we need to light our candles to chase away the darkness that has enveloped our lives. The true meaning of this season is found in the light of hope. Can we rise above our tendencies to be divisive? Is it possible that we could use our light to help heal the differences that keep us from becoming our best selves? Think of the power of millions of candles burning brightly all year long. Light out of darkness, love rising from the ashes of hate, peace overcoming war. Could this be our moment in the sun when those points of light really can stand for something besides shame?

As many of you know I am a huge fan of the late cartoonist Charles Schulz. In the office I have a wonderful "Peanuts" poster of Snoopy slouched across a crescent moon and Woodstock stretched out upon him. The whole scene exudes a sense of tranquility with dazzling golden points of light surrounding the whole scene. Although it is not a Holiday poster per se, it reminds me of the things I wish to remember as December quickly yields to the hard core months of winter. All I really need is some quiet time to reflect, to slow down and to appreciate the wonder of life.

The coming break will allow us all to check out for a week after the hectic weeks of shopping, wrapping and baking.

I wish you days when doing nothing but relaxing is your only goal. Your destination is as close as the most comfortable chair in your home, no ticket required. As the day comes to an end and the darkness replaces the light coming through your windows just remember to do one thing. Instead of automatically switching on an electric light try setting up a few candles. Staring into the flickers of light you will know what it means to experience peacefulness. Maybe the gift of the light is the only thing we need to find our way out of the darkness this year. Just remember, summer absolutely is on the way, the solstice guarantees it! Best wishes for a wonderful New Year and thank you for everything you do to make our school a great place for all of us.

January 3, 2011

Well it is here, the month that seems like it will never end. Last week we endured the snowstorm that promised to remind us that winter in Upstate New York has officially begun and if the magnitude of it was any indication, we are in for a long haul. This year I have resolved to make it a positive month knowing now, more than ever, how quickly time really does pass by. I'll try to seriously put into practice the adage to live every day to the fullest and enjoy the passing of time even as I slog along on trails of ice and newly fallen snow.

Every day certainly is an opportunity to experience one little something or someone that may never come again. So, make this day one of gratitude, growth and wonder at even the starkness of a winter day. If we can live with a determination to honor simplicity our days could indeed match the magic contained in those January sunrises where it looks like someone has taken buckets of gray, orange and pink paints and splashed them across the sky where they have fallen in between puffy clouds to create an abstract mural of instant beauty.

Toni Morrison, a gifted writer who paints gorgeous murals with words reminds us of something very profound. She states, "What every child wants to know is, do your eyes light up when I enter the room? Did you hear me and did what I say mean anything to you"? Given the state of the world as we enter this brand new decade, I think we need to quietly ponder Morrison's wise words. I also believe they apply to adults as well as to children. They are in essence very simple questions that may help to lead us out of the woods of our collective discontent.

It is sometimes easy to take people we see every day for granted. Perhaps we even know their approach by their footsteps and don't even look up to greet them. How many times do we fail to look up from a computer when speaking to a student or colleague? I guess some people would call it the ability to multi-task but I think it is just plain dishonoring. How can you possibly really hear someone, even if they are on the other end of a phone, when you are answering emails? When you are flying on an airplane there is a reason you are instructed to turn off all your electronic devices before take off. All of these gadgets interfere with the plane's navigational systems. So, too, I believe all those things interfere with our own ability to navigate the landscape of another person's need to be heard by us. What ever happened to just giving someone else your complete attention even for the seconds it takes to look up at them? As a human being don't you just want a brief acknowledgement of your very existence?

In order to be able to have your eyes light up when someone enters the room you have to cultivate attention. Clear your head of all of the baggage of the day that has accumulated like old cobwebs and focus on being present. If you are experiencing difficulty with this you can check out any book on Taoism or Zen Buddhism for some tips. Actually, winter is a great time to practice this. Just sit in a quiet room and gaze out a window onto barren tree branches. In the seeming emptiness of this scene know that there is great beauty in dormancy, in the ability of nature to sit out a stretch so she can prepare for the splendor of spring time re-birth. If you can quiet your mind, seek out the stillness, you will be able to use your eyes to light up a hundred rooms. That light will not come through your computer and it will definitely not come at sending a text message. Please don't delude yourself that these devices can replace the ever human need to communicate in person. To do so would only allow us to experience an unending isolation similar to a winter without the promise of spring.

As the days of January tick by remember that you have the ability to change the world one person at a time. Create a fire of warmth for someone this day. Let your eyes glow with the sparks of happiness at the presence of your students, family members, friends, pets and co-workers. The warmth of your presence can literally melt away the coldness that can sting us on these frigid January nights. If that means something to you, then please don't hesitate to gather your kindling.

January 10, 2011

January is usually the month of resolutions. Generally, those resolutions center around some kind of plan to improve our physical well being through a combination of diet and exercise. As often happens, our intentions are sincere but it is in the following through where the problems occur. It seems we all, at some time or another, have shared this burden. I came across a quote recently from George Thornton which addresses this issue. It actually covers a whole range of issues but totally hits a home run on the diet and exercise score.

"Do now what others won't , so later you can do what others can't." It seems odd that we often choose to worry about everything except the only thing that will allow us to live a truly fulfilling life-our health. I think the quote also speaks to other facets of our lives as well. Too often we take the easy way out and just do not want to work hard to achieve a goal. Maybe the problem is that we make our goals unachievable. We shoot for the moon so to speak and then wonder why we end up back where we started with nothing but a sense of disappointment and failure.

The main thing is to concentrate on being people of action. Winter can be an excuse for inaction. It is tempting to sit around neglecting exercise and pretend that we exist in cozy dens like animals hibernating until the first signs of spring appear. However, human biology and that of bears is distinctly different. Whether we care to admit it or not we chose to live in this climate that bequeaths us the gift of four distinct seasons. No doubt about it, winter can be the most challenging of them all. The preponderance of gray skies does not exactly serve to lure us outside for much more activity than fetching the mail. If we subscribe to George Thornton's great statement, though, we will become empowered by helping to shape our physical and mental destiny.

Contrary to popular belief, a 30 minute walk on a cold day can be extremely invigorating. It is not a coincidence that many of society's great thinkers were also committed walkers. Too often we equate exercise with pain, agony and prolific sweating. The benefits of better health actually start by moving your big muscles-in other words walking at a brisk clip. For some people a sensible beginning may be a stroll of five or ten minutes. Unfortunately, if you WON'T begin to help yourself now, pretty soon you will become someone who CAN'T do much of anything without the agony of dependence inching onto your radar screen.

Maybe this is a good time for all of us here at school to make a resolution to each other. We can be comrades in health! Talk to your friends about your fitness adventures. There is a reason that the most successful companies invest in wellness programs for their employees. We are fortunate that the District is getting involved in this area. Share recipes, share fitness strategies and join other classrooms for walks as a recess activity. Don't be someone who, "lives to eat". The latest scientific research is proving that caloric restriction can add years to your life.

Outside the wind may howl and flakes of snow swirl around us as the temperature barely reaches the freezing point. Don't give in but rather throw on an extra layer of soft, cozy fleece and step outside. Granted you might not see too many souls out there on the roads. However, just remember that if you keep up your quest you will surely, in the future, be among a flock of silver crowned geezers who can keep pace with those youngsters who think you CAN'T. So…………
WON'T you join us? As always best wishes for a great week filled with all the twists and turns that working  with kids can provide. It matters to all of us that you chose to show up.

January 24, 2011

I don't normally like to recommend books due to the fact that most readers' tastes widely vary. However, I will gladly violate my own rule to recommend to you a totally thought provoking little book by Andy Andrews, *The Butterfly Effect*. It is something that you will want to purchase and keep handy for the rest of your life. The subtitle is "How Your Life Matters" and it is surely an anecdote for these seemingly endless wintry days of January.

Andy Andrews started off as a successful comedian but he has now become one of the most sought after authors and speakers around today. After reading several of his books I would also characterize him as a brilliant teacher as well. His basic premise is this: "every move we make and every action we take, matters not just for us, but for all of us…and for all time." Truer words were never spoken. These words seem to me to be the absolute foundation for a successful life.

In *The Butterfly Effect* Andrews talks about the original concept by that name and how it was brought up at a conference of scientists in the early 1960's. Edward Lorenz was the originator of the idea that if a butterfly flapped its' wings air would move, moving more air and on the other side of the world a hurricane could begin. Needless to say, Lorenz was considered a fool for thinking in such a unorthodox matter. Fortunately, years later, physics professors proved him right. Lorenz "theory" is now the "law of sensitive dependence upon initial conditions".

The author then goes on to cite a very interesting example of this law in action. During the Civil War a former college professor from Maine was an officer in the Union army. At Gettysburg Joshua Chamberlain was faced with making a decision that would totally effect the outcome of life in the United States the way we know it. Although greatly outnumbered he decided to have his men charge instead of retreat. This maneuver fooled his opponents into scurrying away. The Union, as a result, prevailed and the rest as they say, is history. By making that one decision Chamberlain changed the way we live our lives today in the United States. Would we be living in one country, two, three? The butterfly effect is just that powerful in its' implications.

This is all a perfect example of the importance of individual decision making. Don't for one second think that your life does not matter in the grand scheme of things. You are a complete one of a kind that will never be again, a creation destined for your own special greatness. It is not necessary to move mountains or to be the president or to win an Olympic gold medal. Just be you and know that every word you utter, every decision you make has an effect on someone whether now, or 100 years from now.

For a few minutes think of someone whom you admire and respect. I'll just use Henry David Thoreau as my example. What if Thoreau decided to be a salesman instead of a writer, philosopher and walker? His masterpiece *Walden* probably would never have been written. What if Meryl Streep had chosen to study engineering? Perhaps Abraham Lincoln's mother decided not to have children? What if Rosa Parks just did what she was told? Closer to home we have a staff member who makes exquisite quilts. The detail in them is beautiful and they are truly works of art. I cannot fathom the patience and creativity it takes to complete even one of these quilts. So, Ruth, this one is for you. Who knows in generations to come, where your unique gift could wind up? You will, through a series of actions, have brought happiness to someone, somewhere removed from where you are today. So it will be with every single one of you. It all matters and your presence here matters more than you can ever know.

The Butterfly Effect is a book that should be read to every child from the minute they can comprehend right straight through their entire lifetime. It is so important that each person understand the importance of the message contained within the pages. Sometimes, it really is not all that complicated this life of ours. We obsess, we agonize but in the end it always comes back to those everyday choices.

As I look out the frost encased windows I realize that I will not see those delicate butterfly creatures flittering around. However, as we slowly crawl through these winter days and a few minutes of daylight appear it won't be long before colorful wings flap pushing pockets of air along toward their date with destiny.

March 7, 2011

I can't say that I am a huge fan of Pat Conroy's fiction but his new piece of non-fiction, *My Reading Life*, totally captured my attention. This book allows the reader to reflect on the great questions of life. Along the way Conroy describes the beauty of several parts of the state of South Carolina in prose that is simply stunning.

One of the memorable lines from the book is taken from a discussion of the Japanese word kintsugi. The word means "the Japanese practice of repairing ceramics with gold-laced lacquer to illuminate the breakage". Upon reading this description I kept thinking that these artists really understood how life should be lived. Here was a great example of how in not trying to hide our cracks and flaws we can actually bring them into the light and become better individuals.

Unfortunately, our society is more apt to discard anything that we view as less than perfect. We relegate our flaws to the shadows where we try to either compensate for them or cover them up completely. What if, like those Japanese painters, we filled in our breaks with gold lacquer of patience, gentleness and compassion? It seems to me that our weary world could greatly benefit from a course in psychological kintsugi.

Think about all the children, adults and creatures you come in contact with who could benefit from some kind of repair. Honestly, that could describe any one of us. The culture would have us believe that perfection is the ideal to strive for but perhaps that is a goal not worthy of our effort. Instead maybe we should pick up our brushes and paint away to fill in the damage created by fear, anger, jealousy and greed. In this vein we can all be artists. Look at the cracks of poverty that children in this country are facing due to the recession. Contemplate the growing anger in our political discourse, the brutal words of disrespect and intolerance that are hurled about each day in the media. Our senior citizens who have accumulated decades of wisdom are being cast aside to live out their last years struggling to pay for health care and to live with a dignity they have more than earned. One of the biggest cracks in our collective psyches has to be in the relentless pursuit of money as the capstone of success. We are taught to believe that having gobs of it will make us happy and satisfied beyond measure but this is the biggest myth of them all. Money cannot fix the mess we have created when we shattered a thing called conscience.

In our pursuit of the perfect everything, that we think can outshine everyone, we forget about the only gift that can help another. If we can take the gift of ourselves and paint it onto the breakage of someone else, just maybe we could begin the healing. Time is really all we have and sharing a few moments with a person in need might be our own kintsugi. It is so easy to get caught up in our own little worlds and to exaggerate our own importance. Just showing up, just being there and lending your attention could change the course of the day for someone else. Presence is a wonderful thing to people, pets and even to the natural world. You can fill in the breakage just with your silence sometimes.

This long winter is soon due to break camp and move on even as this first Monday of the month would lead us to believe otherwise. The cold, the snow and ice, the cloudy skies have all served their purpose. Now is the time to look forward in anticipation of better days to come. No doubt they should arrive soon as we all have pretty much reached our breaking points. What a great time to look into the eyes of another and vow to bring out our paintbrushes. Let us paint with thoughts as bright as gold lacquer so that the cracks of our broken spirits can sparkle in the sunshine of a new day.

March 21, 2011

Early Saturday morning I finished a delightful book on writing by Roger Rosenblatt, *Unless It Moves The Human Heart*. The connection to the art of teaching was, for me, undeniable. We have stood by over the last several months to watch just about everyone who is not a teacher attempt to dismiss the profession. A series of charts and graphs is an attempt to quantify what is basically an artistic endeavor into numbers that will supposedly allow the all knowing to evaluate a given teacher.

If this movement succeeds it will destroy the very essence of all that is good about the act of teaching. What really counts is the relationship a teacher is able to establish with a particular student. In other words, it has to move a human heart. It has to move the heart to want to become a seeker of beauty and truth, to slice through all the madness, cruelty and depravity of the human condition to follow the path toward love. Teaching has to lead us all out of the darkness and into the light of knowing ourselves. Only then can we begin to heal the weary world.

This is not to say that sparks of enlightenment will always fly in the classroom. There are many times when facts must be memorized, equations solved and literature deconstructed. Sometimes style will have to come before substance and all sorts of rules must be followed. However, in the grand scheme of things it will be a teacher's desire to touch the heart of another human being that will make the subject matter dance with a contagious spirit that is alive in the best classrooms. How do you chart that? Can you graph the wonder of a first grader who has just made the connection between sounds and letters to unlock the code of language that allows her to read a book to completion? Does the sweat and tears it took the teacher to achieve this feat show up as merely a percentage on a final evaluation? How do you measure awe? We all need to advocate for stopping this insanity before moving the human heart through learning becomes impossible. These little beings before us with hearts just waiting to be moved must not be sacrificed to bureaucracy on our watch. We must still be able to ask, why not, what if?

This week think of ways to challenge yourself and your students to find vehicles to move the human heart. Maybe you will find a story, a poem or a photograph that you can share. I recently saw an unbelievably moving photo from the disaster in Japan. A young woman was separated from her dog and thought he was lost forever. Miraculously the two were reunited and the photo shows the yellow Labrador retriever stretched out on the floor with the woman sleeping

with her head nestled on his back. You do not see her face or eyes but just the top of her dark hair against the dog's light coat. The memory of it became etched in my mind. Sunday morning I was near a small pond where I live and saw a few Canadian geese gliding around the surface where the ice had melted. Suddenly they rose up and their bellies were illuminated by the brilliant newly risen sun. The sheer power of their ascent reminded me of a jetliner lifting off from the tarmac. Only these magnificent creatures did not thunder upward under gallons of fuel but rather gleaned forward silently, seamlessly with the greens and browns of their feathers shining forth, carrying them into a cloudless blue sky. If you were outside late Saturday night and gazed up you may have noticed a full moon charged with extra brilliance due to its' nearness to planet earth. It seemed to outline the dark clouds surrounding it in a glowing halo of white rims.

We must all think of ways, even tiny ways, to be useful to the lives of others. This life we live is not meant to be a solo expedition. The work we do is fundamentally important to the continuation of our species. Continue to believe that the relationships you cultivate in your classrooms, hallways, faculty room, etc. make a difference to all of us.

In these chaotic times we can all feel like boats adrift in a stormy sea. Use the compass of your heart as a beacon of light to guide others safely to shore. More is at stake than you can imagine so navigate well my friends.

May 2, 2011

There is a billboard along interstate 787 sponsored by a health care company. It states, "HEALTHY CHANGES EVERYTHING". No doubt about it, the statement is totally accurate. In this life if you have your health you have the world by the tail. Too often we take this gift for granted. We have managed to over inflate our bodies to accompany our over inflated egos. The results on those matters speak for themselves.

I like the idea of a simple statement to catch people's attention so I have my own idea for a highway billboard. My giant sign would announce, NICE CHANGES EVERYTHING. I can't believe the number of encounters I have had lately where the whole tone was anything but nice. Rude people just seem to have crept into daily life whether they appear on the air waves, the roads, behind sales counters or on the other end of the phone. Television comedy shows too often glorify rudeness as the way to treat other human beings. Making fun of has almost been elevated to an art form.

We want to achieve the status of splendid self actualized show pieces. It seems that we are willing to sacrifice common courtesy and basic manners to cross the finish line first. Self absorption has become our mantra as integrity fades into the background. There is an ever increasing need to stand out, to stand apart from the ordinary in everything from cars to clothing to the way we design our bathrooms and kitchens. Suddenly we all need commercial grade stainless steel stoves and refrigerators even though we eat many of our meals in places outside the home that get us in and out as quickly as possible. Customer service is stunningly absent in the need to keep the herd moving.

But I still believe NICE CHANGES EVERYTHING. I'm not talking about becoming a push over who lets everyone trample all over you. No, I just want to bring back a certain level of civility to life in 2011. As educators of young children it is imperative that we become role models of the NICE CHANGES EVERYTHING philosophy. I am not foolish enough to think that we will click with every single person we come in contact with. Granted, there are some people that can get under your skin in a heart beat. They can bring you to the edge the minute they open their mouth. All too often though, we tend to want to cut them apart with unkind insults. The only thing that this response does is to create another bubble of pain that floats out into an already hurt soaked world. It is time to put the brakes on.

Think of all the little ways we use mean spirited actions and thoughts to cause another person to retreat into a shell of self doubt. It could be as simple as glancing at their choice of clothing or hair style. Maybe you just can't resist making a disparaging comment about a purchase someone made. It is almost as if we say, "I don't want it if you can have it too". Rank used to be reserved for those in the military but not anymore. The self importance ladder just doesn't have enough rungs.

Finally, the rain clouds may be yielding to the glorious days of spring in upstate New York. The yellow green tree buds are poised to explode into newly born leaves. The burst of color makes us smile with gratitude for being allowed to be a witness to the great unfolding of this wonderful season. Let us then make a pact on this dawning day. Lift your head skyward, inhale the scent of all the once a year blossoms that ride on the early spring breeze. Then picture in big white letters blazoned across the deep blue sky, NICE CHANGES EVERYTHING. This is my hope for you and for this weary world as we stand ready to welcome the incredibly beautiful month of May.

May 23, 2011

There are many months that give us something to be grateful for. However, I believe that May is the month that showers us with the finest of nature's many gifts. The April rains left behind a trail of newly carpeted green grass, soft and fine. The first cutting of the lawns smell so fresh that the scent lingers like something so familiar and comforting that everything suddenly feels just right. Tiny violets erupt and remind us that the color purple is dazzling in its brilliance. These little trinkets, gone all too soon, serve notice that life itself is all too brief. Flowering trees in shades of soft pink and white beckon us to come and inhale their aromatic petals. We become creatures of the outdoors again, subjecting our bare skin to the warmth of the sun's penetrating rays.

Indeed the month of May echoes so nicely the words of Leo Tolstoy, "There is no greatness where there is not simplicity, goodness and truth." The question then becomes, why don't we slow down long enough to enjoy the simple gift that May bestows upon us? There is just so much goodness in May. The new growth is everywhere, with the promise of another summer of warmth and abundant sunshine. The month of May makes us believe that we can overturn the soils of winters gloom and plant for ourselves a garden of hope. It kind of seems that hope is in short supply these days. What if we all took the time to till some rows of hope? Perhaps, if we water the soil with kindness and compassion, throw in a few handfuls of fertilizer laced with understanding, the autumn harvest would yield an abundance of goodwill and tolerance for those differences that currently divide us.

Lately, as I look around I see the effects of divisive thinking in all our gardens causing weeds of discontent to all but strangle our newly sprouting seedlings of hope. It is almost impossible to have a civil discourse on anything that matters. We pepper our speech with expletives that have no place in conversations designed to bridge the gap of difference. When talk turns to the need to sacrifice to preserve the common good the biggest weed of them all, fear, winds itself around the roots of our thinking brains taking with it something called common sense. We scurry around like starved mice to hoard everything we think we are entitled to, forgetting that we exist, not as lone wolves, but as members of a greater interdependent community. Can we afford to throw overboard the aged, the infirm, and the truly poor and still call ourselves Americans? When did we accept greed as a national value? How much company profit is enough?

It is easy given our current state of affairs to want to insulate ourselves in a protective cocoon. That might be acceptable as a brief escape but we cannot indulge in such activity for long because we have chosen to call ourselves educators. If we take this mission seriously we must stand firm and help our students to become critical thinkers capable of weeding out empty rhetoric. We need to give them the tools to sensibly debate the important issues without stooping to venom filled speech. The most important tool of all is the ability to become voracious readers. All of the truly great ideas that humankind has developed are present in the works of literature. Novels, poems and works of non fiction contain the code by which we learn how to live an honorable life. Our job is to help students decipher that code so they can seek out their own path to wisdom. The journey begins in kindergarten when the letters and sounds of language gently make their way into the mind's of eager young learners. Hopefully that journey continues right up to the end of life so that we can leave this earthly plane having left behind our own legacy of ideas to guide those that will follow us.

This week, as the vibrant season of spring prepares to yield to the long, lazy days of summer, try to engage a colleague in a conversation of ideas. Leave behind the petty gossip and small talk that consumes our days. Instead, let us see if we can close out this school year walking in a garden of ideas that will challenge us to become people of wisdom and integrity. With the past week of steady, soaking rain our seedling ideas should do pretty well. I would suggest a fertilizer of positive thoughts with maybe a sprinkling of good wishes. The sunshine might be lacking outside but the inside the walls of School 18 those sunbeams of encouragement and hope will be all around you!

June 13, 2011

June is definitely one of my favorite months but it is also one I have a problem with. If you are in the school business it has to be the one you look forward to as the culmination of ten months worth of hard work. In the depths of a January deep freeze thoughts of the arrival of June can surely make a difference to your mental health. However, once the glorious month officially arrives it seems to fly by faster than a sprinter coming off the final turn of a grueling race.

I just want to capture June and stuff it in a knapsack so I can sit under a barren tree in mid November and empty the contents of the sack filled with the scent of fresh picked strawberries, the clean smell of a newly opened swimming pool or the taste of just about anything cooked over glowing coals. But June, you clever little fox, I hardly get to know you before you slither away into those humid days of July. I want to sentence you to extended time before you can be paroled into those lazy days of summer where your gentle breezes all but disappear. June is a thinking person's month. So, before June slips from my grasp I'll leave you with some thoughts to ponder on the summer days ahead.

It is easy to get caught up in judgment. We expend a great deal of time debating the merits of just about everything regarding other people. Unfortunately, we hone our critical thinking skills in the wrong direction. Too much valuable time is spent on finding fault and offering shallow opinions without knowing the background or the true facts of a situation. We all are too quick to judge just about every facet of someone else but we fall short when it comes to getting our own house in order. Maybe we could all find some time this summer to sharpen the saw so we can cut away the old timbers of judgment that prevent us from becoming our best selves. Perhaps this investment of time will lead us to frame a new structure, come September, built on trust and mutual respect.

The other day I was rereading a wonderful book by the photographer/writer Jan Phillips, *Marry Your Muse*. It is a work that celebrates the creative spirit that each one of us possesses. In the early pages Phillips is able to nail down the purpose of our existence when she writes, "Time is all we have. One lifetime under this name to produce a body of work that says, this is how I saw the world". So, what will you do with this palette you are given? How will you create your picture of how you see the world?

As the artist that you are, you can't waste time worrying about what other people are doing, saying or believing. Granted, it is much easier to gossip about someone else than to face the reality of your own existence. That is why negativity is so prevalent in this culture. Artists, however, don't waste their one, precious life entwined in that mess. They are too busy trying to see the world, to capture the essence of what it means to make this earthly journey and to make some kind of sense out of the mystery of it all.

To be an artist is to be a seeker and so we all have artistic talent that needs to be discovered and cultivated. Very few of us will create great masterpieces but all of us need to find some creative outlet that will bring us joy. You might find that creativity in your "day job" or maybe you will fulfill it outside of work. The point is that you must find it in order to understand how you saw the world. It could be as simple as the pleasure you take in creating a beautiful meal for your family and friends. What about the hours you spend in the vegetable garden you planted? Do you keep a journal, write poetry, knit, play a musical instrument just because you can? Are you capable of recognizing wonder?

This might be the time to gather up the timbers of self doubt and set them ablaze. Sit back and watch the sparks fly up into the darkness of the mid June sky and make yourself a promise. Vow to let go of all the judgments of yourself and others that keep you from becoming the artist that is a part of your destiny. Rekindle your true purpose before, as we will ask of the fleeting month of June, where did the time go?

June 20, 2011

I have been thinking lately of the whole concept of self-esteem. Coincidently, there was an article in this month's "Atlantic" magazine that put a different spin on the idea. It was written by a psychotherapist who sees a preponderance of people coming to her office with a rather unique problem.

These people were raised in good households, had normal upbringings, did well in school and had stable relationships. In fact, nothing out of the ordinary occurred in their lives. They entered therapy though, because they were experiencing a general state of discontent and unhappiness. One of the theories raised as to why this malady exists today is that perhaps the twenty-thirty somethings have had it much too good! They are finding it hard to make their way in the world because they have not developed the skills to become independent beings.

The adults who managed to design their "perfect", sheltered, protected lives did nothing to prepare them for the stark realities of the world of 2011. If you have never experienced pain, sickness, death or other kinds of loss, then you have no clue as to how to exist out there in this far from perfect world. Granted, we should shield our children from the many direct images of violence but maybe there has to be a happy median.

Is it possible that in wanting to give children a solid sense of who they are we have created adults who are loaded down with self doubt? Everyone can't be the same wonderful shining star just by the fact that they were born. The problem is that to be truly successful you have to be wiling to put in effort. The key word here is YOU, the singular independent being. Everyone on the team shouldn't get a trophy for simply showing up. If everything is geared toward mediocrity then how do you define excellence?

Another aspect of this situation is in the choice quandary. Why is it necessary to give children a choice in everything from food to social outings? If there is a choice in all situations when you are growing up then how do you function in an adult world where there is not a choice when it comes to being responsible? Showing up at a job at a specific time is not a choice. Doing laundry, keeping yourself clean or living within a budget are things that demand structure. Children who are given a choice all the time in just about everything will have a major meltdown when they are just told what to do. Little kids cannot be given the power to be the kings and queens of their destiny without suffering the mental consequences later on. Why do we need five different kinds of cereal, three kinds of bread or the choice of four dinner entrees in any one household? It seems to me that parents should be more than consultants to the whims of their offspring.

Kids don't need friends for parents they need people with some life experience behind them. The whole idea is to give those children guidance and then set them free to make their own way in the world. Insecurity is not an option any more than dependence should be. Have we made life too comfortable so that even the thought of failure frightens our young people from trying anything new?

Summer vacation is just about here so maybe this is a good opportunity for all of us to take a "time out" and to reflect on these thoughts. We can't continue to be like Linus, the character from "Peanuts" who carries around his security blanket everywhere. These quiet days of summer beckon us to dabble in something a little different. Try something new that challenges you. It could be as simple as attempting a day hike in the mountains. The important thing is to spend some time out of your comfort zone. As a result, the self-esteem you cultivate will be of the genuine kind. In other words, you will have earned it! Happy summer.

About the Author

C.A. Kilgallon has spent the last thirty-two years in the field of elementary education. The last seventeen years she has been a Principal with the Troy City School District.

She continues to have a passion for books and is a voracious reader. Books, as well as observations and critical thinking, become tools for understanding our place in the world.

A first book of essays, Monday Morning Musings was published in 2007.

About the Illustrator

Letitia Monroe is an aspiring graphic artists currently living in New York's Capital Region.

Photo by: Ryan Kilgallon